A BUTCHER'S BOY
ON *Killing, Dying* AND *Death*

Interior of Conrad Bauer's meat market 1897. Conrad Bauer is second from left.

Cover Photo: Conrad Bauer's meat market in Montgomery. Following his marriage to Mary Bury in 1897, they lived in rooms above the meat market. Conrad Bauer is third from left.

A BUTCHER'S BOY
ON *Killing, Dying* AND *Death*

A Memoir

BARTON BAUER

Mill City Press, Inc.
322 First Avenue N, 5th floor
Minneapolis, MN 55401
612.455.2293
www.millcitypublishing.com

Author's note: I have changed some names to protect the privacy of the people involved.

ISBN-13: 978-1-62652-540-5
LCCN: 2013922364

Cover Design by Jenni Wheeler
Typeset by James Arneson
Images courtesy of the Bauer family.

Printed in the United States of America

*To my wife Shirley, our three sons Jeff, Scott and Brent and their families.
You've made my life worth living.*

TABLE *of* CONTENTS

Acknowledgments

OVER THE YEARS, I HAVE read a number of books: novels, short stories, biographies, and some written by people about themselves. In the 1960s, I thought about trying my hand at writing. I took a night course on writing fiction and started a novel based on my experiences in the Philippine Islands as a U.S. Navy weather observer. I never got beyond a few pages. It was difficult and besides I was too busy with my job, my family, and my community responsibilities. That was my excuse to quit.

Then, thirty years later and after my father died, I stumbled upon a book given to my wife, Shirley, in 1984 by a 62-year-old patient at the medical clinic where she worked as a receptionist. His name was Floyd Atchison and his book was entitled "A Hole in the Curtain." It was an unpublished account of his life growing up in extreme poverty in a small Mississippi River town during the Great Depression of the 1930s. He'd had limited education, having quit school at age 16, and had made his living laying carpet. Although the book was not well organized and needed much editing, it was a heartfelt story he wanted to share with his children and grandchildren. I thought it a wonderful gift to leave to his family. I thought if he could do it, I could too.

Floyd Atchinson is gone now. He died in 1988 at age 67. I still have his book, and his words and inspiration live on with me. So Floyd, wherever you are—thank you.

And thanks to Barbara Haselbeck, my editor, who made this book possible.

Prologue – 2010

As I start the story of my early years, I wonder if I will see it through. I am 78 years old, stooped over from compression fractures of my spine. Osteoporosis has reduced my height three inches—from 5'10" to 5'7". But my mind is still good and I am determined.

As I look back over my life it seems to have been separated into two distinct parts: The first as a butcher's son—my father a partner in a small-town meat market in rural South Central Minnesota. The second, as a soldier in the trenches of government. The differences so extreme, one can hardly imagine.

My growing up years were dominated by my father. Although I was close to my mother, my dad held the power; he was the authority figure I tried so hard to please—until the final break.

Even today, 16 years after he died, I think of my father's life and death and how he died. And it brings to mind how my other relatives died—and makes me wonder how I will die.

I was with my dad just before the end came and I made a fatal decision—a decision I have thought about many times. Would I do the same thing if I could do it again? I don't know. Did I do right? You be the judge.

I. FATHERS *and* SONS

1.

Death—Its Mystery

I KILLED MY FATHER. I did not know it then, but I know it now. I was his Dr. Kevorkian. I did not mean it, it wasn't my intention, but that's what happened. And all I wanted to do was help him.

It was 10 a.m. on August 5, 1994. Dad was in bed in his room at the Mala Strana Health Care Center in New Prague, Minnesota with an oxygen mask clamped on his face, his chest heaving to get air, his eyes darting wide with fear. He was suffocating and he knew it. My mother and I were sitting near his bed wanting to do something, anything to help, but we didn't know how.

My father was 91 years old, his lungs ravaged from a lifetime of smoking Chesterfield non-filter cigarettes. His physician diagnosed his condition as pulmonary fibrosis—the onset sudden. In May 1993, on his 90th birthday, Dad blew out all his candles. Several months later, however, shortness of breath set in. He had to rest after walking just 100 feet from the house to his garage where he tinkered on a workbench. Then came an oxygen tank near his bed, and finally in April 1994, when Mom could no longer care for him—the nursing home.

Looking back, I wonder why I did not go to him, take his hand, say I loved him, or at least offer some words of comfort. But I didn't and neither did my mother. We just sat there, watching him fight for life.

That was, however, the nature of our family. I never saw Dad embrace Mom, never saw them kiss, never heard the words "I love you." I can't recall my father ever putting an arm around me, or saying much to me. He kept his feelings to himself.

But then I never saw my grandfather, Conrad Bauer, my Dad's father, ever show his feelings—except for anger; then it was okay to rant and rage. Perhaps it was a German thing—keeping feelings of affection to oneself.

However, I do know that my father wanted solace in his last days. A week or so before his death, he asked me to have "Tom" come to him. Who was Tom, I wondered?

I found out later that Tom was often called to come to the room of patients in distress—particularly those near death. Tom was only an aide at the care center—not a chaplain—but he had the gift. He would hold their hands, pray with them, and offer words of comfort. Looking back, I suspect my father would have rather had Tom with him than Mom or me.

As I watched Dad struggle for air, I knew I had to do something. I was trained to help. I had a master's degree in social work, had counseled mental patients in a state hospital, and had advised welfare recipients at a county agency. Four years before, I had retired after 30 years with the Minnesota Department of Human Services. This was my father who needed me—I owed him that. But reaching out with more than a handshake was beyond me. Even to my own sons, a hug did not come naturally—nor to my father.

Then a thought came—morphine. Morphine might help. Help to alleviate Dad's anxiety, reduce the fear, help him to breathe.

Morphine is an analgesic, derived from the opium poppy, and often used to treat severe pain. Less than a year before, I had seen its beneficial effect on a dying person. My aunt Esther Bauer, Dad's 88-year-old sister, was dying of lung cancer at home under hospice care. Her primary caregiver was her 83-year-old sister Dorothy

Bauer. The two were inseparable, neither ever having married, and had lived together most of their adult lives in St. Paul. Both were well educated with degrees from the University of Minnesota.

As a nephew, and a retired social worker living less than 20 miles from my aunts, it was natural I offered to help Dorothy with Esther's care—and she readily accepted. I tried to get over to the house each day to help Dorothy with shopping and to spend time with Esther.

The hospice physician had ordered morphine to be given Esther on a regular basis. I took the prescription to a St. Paul hospital pharmacy and got a full bottle of liquid morphine. Then Dorothy and I filled a host of small syringes with the proper dosage.

Esther had been spending her time propped up in bed, reading and writing. As first Esther did not want the morphine. She thought it would confuse her mind. But when the pain grew too much, she took the syringe and squirted the fluid into her mouth. I asked her how she felt. Esther smiled, a dreamy look came over her face, and she made gentle wave-like motions with her hand to indicate a pleasant euphoria had taken hold. From that time on she welcomed each syringe.

I was with Esther the day she died. I had come to the house that morning to help Dorothy and see how Esther was doing. For days we expected death to be imminent. Esther was no longer taking food or drink and spent most of the time sleeping. We continued the morphine, however, brushing small amounts in her mouth and gums.

When I came in, Dorothy was in the kitchen. She said Esther was comatose and no longer responsive. She asked me to take Esther's bible, go into her room and read to her. She thought if Esther could still hear, it would be a comfort to her.

I went into Esther's darkened bedroom. She was lying propped up in bed, eyes closed as if deep in sleep. I pulled up a chair near her bed and sat down. I opened Esther's Bible. There was a book-marker placed in the Old Testament's Book of Proverbs. The Book of Proverbs is a collection of the sayings of the sages of Israel, a large portion ascribed to King Solomon. I leafed through and noticed Esther had underlined or highlighted many of Solomon's wise guidelines for living. I assumed she must have found these words helpful in her own life.

I began reading aloud the highlighted parts. Although Esther made no response, I continued for about 15 minutes. Then Esther made a soft sound I can't describe. I went to her bed and noticed she had stopped breathing. I walked into the kitchen and told Dorothy I thought Esther had passed away. Dorothy, without showing emotion, went in and confirmed it was so.

I thought Esther died the "good" death—without fear or pain. Morphine had worked for Esther, perhaps it would work for my father. Hoping to relieve Dad's anxiety and ease his breathing, I called the nurse and asked if he could have morphine. She checked his chart and said the doctor had so ordered. She brought a small vial of morphine and offered it to my father. He drank and seemed to relax, to breathe more easily.

About 11:30, my mother and I decided to go to the nearby hospital and have lunch in the cafeteria. Shortly after the noon hour we returned to the nursing home. A nurse rushed up to us in the hallway and said my father had just died. She said they were feeding him soup and he passed away. We went to his room. He was lying on his back, his body at peace, his futile fight for air over.

Looking back, the dose of morphine probably finished my father. Feeding him soup, however, when he had trouble breathing couldn't have helped—too easy for it to go down the wrong way, for Dad to choke on it. But the morphine, I'm convinced, brought on the end.

We called the funeral director in Montgomery to come for my father's body. While we waited, Mom and I just looked at Dad, moon-faced, his body flaccid from prednisone, a steroid he'd been taking for his condition. We said little, lost in our own thoughts. Although we expected his death, when it came it was hard to believe. To me, my father was always so full of life—with energy I could never approximate. Now it was over, and soon his body would be committed to the earth.

Within an hour or so, the funeral director came, placed my father's body in a clear plastic bag and zipped it up. As the funeral director wheeled Dad's body down the hall and into the hearse waiting in the back of the nursing home, I thought back to when I was a kid, how much I wanted to be like "Pa"—my father. (To my mother and younger brother my father was Pa.).

My father was a butcher, and I wanted to be a butcher too. And when Dad wasn't working, he was hunting—raccoon and fox—and was considered one of the best hunters in the county. I wanted to be good at hunting too. And I thought of how he loved his dogs—sometimes, I think, more than he loved people. I wanted to be my father's son. I wanted his love and respect.

My first recollection of helping my father in the butcher business was when I was about five years old. It was 1937, the height of the Great Depression. We were in the back of our meat market on Main Street in Montgomery, a town of about 1900 people in Minnesota, 50 miles southwest of the Twin Cities.

My father was butchering a calf he had purchased from a farmer. The farmer brought the calf in his pickup truck all trussed up to the back room of the meat market.

I watched Dad and the farmer lift the calf from the truck box and lay it on a wooden bench. The calf's legs were bound together with rope so tightly it could only move its head. Then my father handed me a small pail and a foot-long wooden ruler. "Bart, hold the pail under the calf's throat and catch the blood." He poured a small handful of salt into the pail. "And keep stirring so it won't clot." I learned later the blood would be used in making blood sausage.

I was nervous as I watched Dad reach for a skinning knife. Suddenly the calf struggled and bawled for its mother, its eyes rolling in terror. In one swift motion, Dad grabbed the calf's jaw, pulled its head back, and slashed the throat from ear to ear. As the calf's body jerked at the knife cut, then strained against the ropes, I quickly got the pail under the fountain of blood gushing out and began stirring.

Even as the calf's chest heaved, drawing air that wheezed through its severed windpipe—it was the animal's eyes that held me. As the blood flow slowed to a thin gentle stream, the calf's eyes stopped rolling and looked steadily into mine; then softened, as if no longer afraid. The body relaxed. Slowly the eyes lost their focus and glazed over. It was my first vague glimmer of the mystery, the finality of death.

For the next 14 years, until I joined the U.S. Navy during the Korean War, I was a willing assistant to my father in the butcher business. Bauer's Meat Market was one of three butcher shops in town. Just about every day we killed something to meet the needs of our customers: cattle, hogs, and chickens.

The work was arduous and dirty. We slaughtered cattle in a one-room unheated slaughterhouse. In winter, wearing blood encrusted coveralls, we kept our hands warm handling steaming entrails. In summer, we worked bare-chested when scalding hogs.

Killing and death was our job—the sights and sounds so appalling we never encouraged anyone to watch us. Once, by accident, a salesman came out to the slaughterhouse to see Dad and left after getting sick at the sight of all the blood. We were a killing machine and I grew adept. By the time I was in high school, I could skin the carcass of a steer almost as fast as Pa. I found I could slash the throat of a chicken and snap its neck: 20 chickens within five minutes.

Like my father, in time, I became inured, my sensitivities callous to the sight, sounds, and smell of death: the gush of arterial blood from slashed throats, the flailing of legs and hoofs in final death throes, and the stench of feces and urine released at the last gasp. Maybe it was in our DNA, inherited from the patriarch of our trade, my grandfather Conrad Bauer.

July 22, 1938 South St. Paul Market Reporter: Things were quite different at the "stockyards" at South Saint Paul in 1887 when Conrad Bauer of Montgomery Minnesota, shown at the left above, first began shipping livestock. There were no big packing plants here then. Only a few scattered pens were noted where since has been erected the big modern stockyards. Mr. Bauer is still active and has seen the great change that has taken place here at the yards as he has been a livestock shipper ever since those early days. With him at South St. Paul a few days ago were his son, Milton Bauer, right, and his grandson, Barton Bauer.

Three Generations Visit Yards

Things were quite different at the "stockyards" at South St. Paul back in 1887 when Conrad Bauer of Montgomery, Minnesota, shown at the left above, first began shipping livestock. There were no big packing plants here then. Only a few scattered pens were noted where since has been erected the big modern stockyards. Mr. Bauer is still active and has seen the great change that has taken place here at the yards as he has been a livestock shipper ever since those early days. With him at South St. Paul a few days ago were his son, Milton Bauer, right, and his grandson, Barton Bauer.

2.

Grandpa Conrad

I ONLY KNEW GRANDPA Conrad as an elderly man—the last eleven years of his life. I remember him as well built with gray hair, a full mustache and a commanding presence. He reminded me of a retired army general. When taking a trip, his clothes were like a uniform: a brown suit, vest with pocket watch and chain and a felt hat. He used a cane more as a badge of authority than as a crutch on which to lean—walking with head up and back straight.

He was born in Zuffenhausen (near Stuttgart) in Germany on March 22, 1864, the second of seven children, to Konrad and Katherine (Schaeffer) Bauer, owners of a small farm of 22 acres. Knowing that his older brother Jacob stood to inherit the farm, my grandfather and his younger sister Pauline struck out for America in 1887 to seek their fortune.

Grandpa Conrad and Pauline landed in the pioneer town of Montgomery (named in honor of Revolutionary War hero General Richard Montgomery): a handful of general stores, blacksmiths, boot and harness shops and saloons, located in the extensive forest know as "The Big Woods," in south central Minnesota. Between 1856 and 1860, a number of Czech, German and Irish families had settled in the area.

From all accounts, my grandfather was a driven man. His dream was to be a butcher so he went to St. Paul, the capitol city, and worked for a sausage maker at $10 a month to learn the trade. Two years later, in 1889, he returned to Montgomery and opened a meat market.

Grandpa Conrad worked hard to establish himself. Then, eight years later, at age 33, he married Mary Bury, a 29-year-old manager of a novelty store in town. It must have been a perfect choice for a man burning with ambition. Grandma Mary was no young girl with her head filled with romantic notions; she was a proven businesswoman. And she spoke German, an important consideration in a town filled with Bohemian immigrants.

My grandmother's people were German-speaking Swiss who came to Minnesota in the 1850s and settled on land owned by the railroad in what was to become Montgomery township. They were farm folks whose plan was to sink roots and become good Americans. And they proved their loyalty in a heart felt way. When the U.S. Civil War broke out in 1861, Grandma Mary's father, his four brothers and a nephew, joined the Union cause. One brother and the nephew died of wounds and disease, as soldiers in the conflict.

My grandparents had five children that lived beyond early infancy: Carl (born 1898), William (1900), Milton (1903), Esther (1905) and Dorothy (1907).

The death of Carl, the first born, was truly tragic. A loveable little boy, he died of diphtheria in 1899, just before he began to walk. His body was taken to the cemetery on a horse-drawn sleigh by men wearing facemasks to protect them from the contagious disease. Grandma, who was not allowed to follow to the cemetery (perhaps because of her exposure to the disease), frequently related the terrible pain of a mother's grief as she watched the burial sleigh take her little boy away.

Upon marriage, Grandma Bauer followed the German code for the housewife: Kuche, Kinder, Kirche (kitchen, children, church) and gave up the store. She was strong in her religious faith and taught Sunday school at St. John Lutheran Church in Montgomery.

In 1923, my grandmother was found to have advanced cancer of the "female organs." During the painful months of sickness, she remained at home spending hours reading the Bible.

During the last hours of agony, she sang old favorite church hymns. Grandmother's death on February 11, 1924, at age 56 was not considered untimely. Her teenage daughters, Esther and Dorothy, were consoled at the funeral by well-meaning church women who said, "Your mother has lived a long and good life."

My grandfather never remarried. He devoted the rest of his life to making his business a success.

Grandpa Conrad held three tenants: work hard, be thrifty and buy land—and he taught by example. Grandpa's waking hours were consumed by work. He went to the meat market at 6 a.m. to cut meat and be ready for customers by 7 a.m.. The shop was open until 6 p.m. Monday through Friday, and until 10 p.m. on Saturdays. On Sundays he opened after morning church for several hours. Evenings often found him making sausage or butchering cattle, pigs, or chickens for the meat counter—sometimes until midnight or 1 a.m. and too tired to take off his clothes before going to bed.

If anyone in the family showed laziness, Grandpa cautioned, "You will end up in the poor house." And if a person did not work and was indigent, he could end up on the county poor farm, cleaning floors and doing other menial tasks for food and a place to sleep.

And he was thrifty. When my mother bought toilet paper, Grandpa told my brother Milt and I to use just one square of paper from the roll each time we went to the bathroom—that was enough to get the job done!

Another example of my grandfather's frugality was the meat choices our family had for meals. You would think owning a meat market would mean we would enjoy the best cuts of beef and pork, but no—I can't recall eating a T-bone steak or a beef or pork tenderloin, but I do remember Bologna "baloney" sausage, wieners, hamburger, and ox-tail soup. The most expensive cuts were saved for the wealthy customers.

Real estate was the most important asset to own in Grandpa's mind. Buildings and farmland were his chief investments. His saying was that you can't grow land; there is just so much in this world. The more people that come to this country, the more valuable it will become.

My grandfather was a shrewd businessman. At the time of his retirement, Conrad Bauer and Sons owned several farms in the Montgomery area, financial interest in the Alba Hotel (now the Monty Hotel) an apartment building (called the "flat"), and the meat market—all in Montgomery. He also owned stock in Swift and Company (a meat packing company in South St. Paul), the Citizen's State Bank (the only bank in town and of which he was a director) the Minnesota Valley Canning Company (which in 1950 became the Green Giant Company) and 60 shares in the Montgomery Brewing Company. Most of these assets were acquired through Grandpa's business acumen.

Some people in town said my grandfather wasn't entirely honest. As a boy I heard stories, said in some jest, that on occasion he weighed his thumb when putting meat on the scale; and that he could be a little shady when buying cattle from farmers.

Although sensitive to these tales of questionable dealings, Grandpa understood their origin. His answer was "when your head is above the crowd, some people will throw rocks at it." In other words, success begets envy.

Language also created a problem for my grandfather. Many of the "Bohemian" people spoke only Czech in their homes and German folks spoke German. When I entered first grade in

Montgomery Public School (1938), about five of the 20 in my class could speak little English—only Czech. In our home, English was spoken because Dad (German) and Mom (Czech) could not communicate in one another's ancestral tongue. (Unfortunately for my brother and I, neither of us learned a second language because of this).

Grandpa spoke broken English. I can recall older Bohemian boys mocking my grandfather by mimicking his disjointed English— "Milton, throw the cows over the fence some hay"—they would say. Milton (his son) was my Dad.

Being of German heritage in a small American town during World War I and II didn't help. During the First World War there were fundraisers to increase money for the war effort. Each businessman in Montgomery was expected to donate some item for a town auction sale. Grandpa donated a prize yearling heifer—the most valuable donated gift of any businessman in town. This was done to show his loyalty to the United States.

Like many Germans, Grandpa liked alcoholic spirits. Before Prohibition, Montgomery had a brewery to which he would send a boy to get a bucket of beer. The bucket was kept in the meat market with a dipper. He drank beer during the day instead of water—saying water was good only to take a bath or to water the livestock.

When Prohibition ended in 1933, Grandpa liked to walk the six blocks from home to the Alba Hotel and Saloon for a few beers. When he became to old and crippled with rheumatism, he would talk Mom into driving him to the saloon (he never learned to drive a car), giving her a handful of nickels to play the slot machines (they were legal in saloons then) so she would be entertained while he enjoyed his beer.

Although loyal to the United States, Grandfather never lost his love for his native land. Toward the end of World War II,

German prisoners of war were brought to a prison camp next to the Minnesota Valley Canning Company in Montgomery. The factory canned sweet corn and peas (under the Green Giant label) grown on fields in the area. The German prisoners were used to pick corn in the fields—filling horse-drawn wagons for the factory. When not working in the fields, the prisoners were interned in barracks surrounded by a high fence. In the evening, on occasion, mother would drive Grandpa to the camp in my father's 1941 Chevrolet to visit the prisoners. There, in the German language in which he was most comfortable, Grandpa would talk to prisoners from his "home" area in Germany and inquire about conditions in the fatherland.

In the last days of his life Grandfather rarely left the house, but he did have visitors. One in particular stands out: George Brunner—a vigorous German-born man in his mid seventies who lived about four blocks away. In the early afternoon I would see Mr. Brunner marching down the sidewalk toward our house; back straight, eyes forward like a soldier on parade—swinging his walking stick in cadence with his step. Grandfather would be sitting in his usual place: a rocking chair in the kitchen next to the wood stove, smoking a cigar or pipe. Mr. Brunner would be welcomed in, have a chair next to Grandpa, and together they would discuss the news of the day—in German. Mr. Brunner, an excitable man, talked without cessation, voice rising as he gesticulated wildly with his arms to make a point. Grandpa listened, occasionally responding to keep the conversation going.

I never knew what they talked about, but once Mr. Brunner lead them in prayer, and another time they sang, with faces flushed, patriotic German songs—one song I learned later was Deutschland Über Ales.

Grandfather was not anti-Semitic. He sold his interest in the Alba Hotel to a Jewish man from out of town. There never had been Jews in Montgomery. When questioned about selling to a Jew, Grandpa simply said: "I sold to him because he is a good businessman." To Grandpa that was what counted.

Although Grandpa had the reputation of being a tough old German, I got along fine with him. I was quiet and reserved as a boy and I did what I was told to do. I did chores for him: going to the store for his pipe tobacco and carrying wood for the stove to keep him warm. When I was little, he called me "Das kleine Mann"—German for the little man.

Conrad Bauer, his wife Mary, and their children, about 1911 or 1912: Children from left Esther, Dorothy, William, and Milton (my father)

This photo was part of a Christmas card sent by Esther and Dorothy Bauer in 1937. The photo, taken in 1912, shows the four children of Conrad Bauer in a cornfield. From left are Esther, Dorothy in cart filled with corn, pulled by a goat with William holding it by a chain, and Milton, my dad, holding onto the dog.

Conrad Bauer's house at 502 Oak Ave. W in Montgomery, built about 1898—and still stands

Conrad Bauer in early 1940s. In front of Esther
and Dorothy Bauer's house on 229 Macalester
Street in St. Paul.

3.

The Rivalry

MY FATHER MILTON and Uncle Bill were born at the turn of the century: Bill in 1900 (the same year President William McKinley was re-elected on a "full dinner-pail" platform), and Dad almost three years later.

As boys, both Dad and Uncle Bill loved outdoor activities: hunting and trapping; but were less than enthusiastic about school. This attitude was not unusual in a farm community in those days when a boy went to school until he could do a "man's work"— usually about 14 years of age. Consequently, they quit school after finishing eighth grade.

Grandpa Conrad thought a boy should go to school until he could read, write, and "figure"; after that it was time to go to work. An example of Grandfather's attitude was illustrated by a story my father's sister (Aunt Dorothy) told: It was a school day; my father was in the 8th grade; it was harvest time on the farm; and every hand was needed. Grandpa stormed into the school classroom; confronted my father's teacher, saying, "the boy has had enough school, there is work to be done," and over the teacher's protest, took Father out of school—much to the embarrassment of his younger sisters, Esther and Dorothy.

Grandfather was very strict and demanded hard work from all his children—particularly Bill. When Bill was in his late teens, he left home and went to South Dakota to live and work with relatives there. After a year or so, he returned and resumed work with Grandpa in the meat market.

Father and Uncle Bill were different: physically, and in their personalities. Dad was about five feet seven inches in height, wiry, and never varied in weight of 145 lbs until the last years of his long life of 91 years. He was considered handsome, with wavy brown hair and hazel eyes, and quite a "lady's man" before his marriage to mother. He was something of a loner and preferred to work alone. Although he "partied" as a single man, after marriage he rarely drank alcoholic beverages.

Uncle Bill, on the other hand, was several inches taller than Dad and heavier built. He was gregarious and something of a "sport" in town. He loved baseball, boxing, and hunting. An ardent follower of the town baseball team, he usually bet a little money on the outcome of each game. When it came to boxing, he was a true fan. His favorite fighter was Joe Louis, the world heavyweight champion during the 1930s and 40s, and on whom he bet and won several large wagers.

As Father and Uncle Bill grew up, there developed a certain rivalry between the two brothers. They competed in raccoon hunting (who got the most coon in a season, and who had the best coon hound), and in work. Different in personality and with different friends, they never hunted or worked together. Though business partners, they managed to separate their responsibilities completely. Bill stayed in the shop front room serving customers; and Dad in the back room making sausage and running the farm and slaughtering operation.

There was an unspoken understanding that each stay out of the other's "territory." That understanding may have come after a confrontation between the two young men in the sausage room. On this occasion, Dad was hanging strings of freshly made sausage in the smoke house on five-foot-long "smoke sticks." These smoke sticks were almost twice the thickness of a broomstick, and heavier. Bill came to the back room for some reason and an argument developed that led to a shouting match. Dad, temper out of control, grabbed a smoke stick and went after Bill. Surprised, Bill took another stick and fought back. Like two ancient swordsmen they battled until Bill gave in and retreated to his domain—the front room. Fortunately, there were no reports of injury.

This estrangement carried over into social affairs. Although living next to one another, my father and Uncle Bill never visited, or entertained on Christmas or other holidays. I can't recall ever seeing the two of them together for any event.

In 1923, Uncle Bill married and built a house next to Grandpa Conrad. Two daughters were born to this union: Annabelle and Mary.

I remember the first time I got drunk. I was an usher at Mary's wedding; I was 17 years old. There was a reception at a nearby nightclub in the afternoon following the wedding. The bar was open, the beer and whiskey free, and he bartender never asked for an ID as long as you held your liquor "like a man."

Don G., a well build 28-year-old member of the wedding, motioned me to an empty chair next to him at the bar and asked, "What are you drinking, Bart? I'll order."

I wasn't accustomed to drinking hard liquor—a beer or two at most was usually my limit—but with bravado I replied, "Whatever you're having."

Don, well known for his ability to hold his liquor, was drinking whiskey sours, a popular highball at the time.

I planned to have one or two drinks before the wedding dinner, then be ready for the wedding dance that evening. The dance would be in the old Downtown Hall on Main Street and open to the public. My high school friends planned to meet me there for a night of fun.

In high spirits, Don was joking, telling stories—and drinking fast, perhaps to get his share of the free drinks before the bar closed. Before his glass was empty, he hand signaled the bartender to bring us both fresh drinks. The drinks were strong, close to two shots of whiskey to a highball, and I wasn't keeping up. Highballs were stacking up in front of me, and a "real man" never walked away and left a drink stand.

About two hours later, the call came for dinner. I had a half empty drink in hand, and a full one in front of me. I finished my drink in a gulp and got up to go to the restroom.

"You're not going to leave that fresh one stand, are you?" Don questioned.

I was matching a guy with a "rep", drink for drink, and felt pretty cocky. Besides I wasn't feeling the alcohol that much and rose to the challenge. "Nah, that would be a real sin," I replied, and chugalugged the last one down.

In the men's room addressing the urinal, it hit me. The walls started spinning around. Dizzy, I tried to hold onto the wall, but the room kept moving. I tried to walk to the door, and fell into a corner. I struggled to get up, but couldn't.

Word got to Mary's new husband, and he got help. With a man on each side they hoisted me up. Then with my legs noodles, and my shoes dragging behind, I was carried out the men's room, past a row of booths (one with my parents), out the nightclub door, and into a car. Someone took me home and put me to bed—at 6:30 p.m, For me the party was over!

The next day I got a terrible ribbing from my high school friends.

My parents said nothing. Did they see my humiliation? I'm not sure. If they did, Dad's thinking went something like this: "The kid's got to learn how to drink sooner or later. Best he learn among people who care and will look out for him."

I did learn valuable lessons: treat alcohol with respect—and a real man is not determined by the amount of liquor he can drink!

4.

Mom and Dad—Tying the Knot

MY MOTHER WAS born the only child to James and Mary Holey on August 26, 1911, on a farm near Montgomery. She attended a two-room country school until third grade when the family moved into town and rented a house on Main Street. She went to the high school in Montgomery through sophomore year, quitting school at age 16 years to start work as a clerk.

Mother was a pretty girl, slender with brown hair and an angelic face. During the fall of 1930, she was one of five "Kolacky Girls" forming a Montgomery delegation to the state capitol in St. Paul that met with Governor Floyd B. Olson to promote the celebration of Kolacky Day, Montgomery's annual Czech festival. Wearing native Bohemian costumes, they charmed him into eating a kolacky bun.

Along with being pretty, Mother had a soft and gentle nature. Any suffering person or animal was sure to bring forth from Mom a sigh, a gentle nod of the head, and the words "that poor thing." A friend's illness or a sad movie could easily bring her to tears. Her every word and action seemed prompted by a desire to please, or avoid offense to someone. Her docile temperament and willingness to follow a strong lead seemed a perfect complement to the Bauer family traits and father's personality.

All through life, Mother seemed controlled by others: as a child by her mother; after marriage by Dad—which led to a fatalistic attitude. When someone died, lost a job, got sick with a fatal disease, or had a marriage go bad, Mom's usual comment was: "Well, that's the way it goes" or "It's all in the game."

Mom and Dad grew into adulthood and started dating during the "Roaring Twenties" and prohibition. Although the manufacture and sale of liquor was illegal, seldom was there a wedding dance when some alcohol was not consumed—often in the form of "moonshine," an illegally distilled corn whiskey. Dad told about bootleggers in the Montgomery area that had stills in the woods. All the young swains knew who to see to buy moonshine before the big dance.

The 1920s and prohibition spawned the gangster era. As a young man, Dad and a friend took an auto trip through the Midwest to California. On the way they stopped in Wichita, Kansas and checked into a hotel. Shortly after they were shocked when cops burst through the door and with guns drawn, shouted, "reach"! After a brief interrogation they were released. It seemed the police thought they were bank robbers from out of town.

After dating for almost three years, father married mother on April 4, 1932. Because Mom had been confirmed Catholic, the wedding was held in the St. John Lutheran Church parsonage (the house provided by the church for its pastor). Later Mom took "instructions" and converted to Lutheranism.

For their honeymoon in 1932, Dad and Mom went to Chicago. A friend from Montgomery, living in Chicago, took them to a "speakeasy" (an illegal nightclub). While they were there, a "hat was passed" for a donation for the funeral of Red and Ernie: two hoodlums killed during a gang war. With the friend's prudent suggestion, Dad made a conspicuous display of throwing in two dollars.

After marrying they moved into an apartment building (the "flat") owned by Grandpa Conrad and located just off the main street in Montgomery.

For Mom and Dad the Roaring Twenties were over—and hard times were at hand.

Aunt Dorothy Bauer, Milton Bauer, and Paul Ehmke in 1923–24. Dad was about 20 or 21 years old and Dorothy 16 or 17.

Mother as Kolacky Day princess, 4th from left, in St. Paul with local dignitaries about 1930.

Milton Bauer and Rose Holey were married on April 4, 1932

Dad and Mom (left).

My father at Grandpa and Grandma Holey's farm in early 1933 (middle).

On the farm of my grandparents James and Mary Holey in early 1933. From left, Grandma Mary, Mom and I (the baby), the calf, and Grandpa Jim (lower).

My father Milton Bauer with a meat saw and a .22 rifle behind Grandpa
Conrad Bauer's house at 502 Oak Ave. W. in Montgomery in the 1930s

My Uncle Bill Bauer, two hired men, Clayton Dvorak and Miles (Lindy)
Linberger, my father Milton Bauer in front of Bauer's Meat Market on
Main Street in the early 1940s. Ann Bauer, Bill's wife, is at left.

William (Bill) Bauer (Conrad Bauer's oldest child and my uncle) standing in his butcher's apron in the back of Bauer's Meat Market in the early 1940s.

II. HARD TIMES

5.

Depression Days

THE WORLD OF MY birth in 1932 was a world writhing in agony in the midst of the Great Depression. The stock market crash in 1929 left the economy in shambles, prices collapsed, and unemployment was widespread with 12 million out of work in the United States. Mortgages were foreclosed on thousands of homes and farms. Bank failures swept away savings.

In desperation the country searched for a new leader, and found one in the election of Franklin Delano Roosevelt as the 32nd president of the United States. In his inaugural address on March 4, 1933, President Roosevelt sought to rally the country by beginning with the words: "First of all let me assert my firm belief that the only thing we have to fear is fear itself—nameless, unreasoning, unjustified terror."

The economic disaster was only one of the many ways 1932 was different from today. For instance, the average prices throughout the country in 1932 for the following items are enlightening:

Average income	$1,652
New car	$610
New house	$6,515
Loaf of bread	$.07
Gallon of gas	$.10
Gallon of milk	$.43

My town, Montgomery, with a main street of six blocks and a population of about 1900, was affected by the Great Depression, but not as badly as the big cities. We were a farm community that grew a good share of our own food. Just about every family, whether living in town or on a farm, had its own garden, with tomatoes, potatoes, onions, cabbage, and carrots being common crops. Everyone it seemed had an apple tree.

And what food wasn't grown was hunted, trapped, or fished. Pheasant, duck, rabbit, and squirrel were abundant in the wooded farm country and provided the main entrée for many a meal. You could drive out of Montgomery in any direction and within three or four miles run into one or more lakes, providing bullhead, carp, sheepshead, crappie, sunfish, and pickerel that could be fished or speared nine months of the year.

Autumn was the best time of year for food as well as weather, the time when gardens and trees bore fresh vegetables and fruit, and when hunters brought home meat for the pot. What wasn't eaten fresh was canned, smoked, or pickled for eating the rest of the year. Some families bought little food other than basic staples (flour, lard, sugar, salt, and pepper), and literally lived off the land. Somehow, most families made do.

But food was not the only necessity, or expense. Minnesota winters were long and cold. Warm housing was required with mortgage or rent to be paid; wood, coal, or oil had to be purchased to heat the house; and the need for warm clothing and boots could not be ignored. And then there were doctor bills—in those rare instances when a physician was called.

That meant the father, the head of the house and sole bread-winner, needed a job—any job. To be unemployed in Montgomery in those days was not looked upon as sympathetically as it is today. If you were not working, it was your fault, not society's. With no welfare office to go to for help, you went hat in hand to relatives and friends.

People had no experience in looking to government for help. And when the Work Progress Administration (WPA), a federal program, was passed into law in 1935 providing public work for the unemployed, the odd jobs (raking leaves, building sidewalks and playgrounds, etc.) and the men who took them were looked upon with derision. WPA became "We Poke Along" and the men who worked the jobs were laughed at as spending most of the day leaning on a rake or shovel.

Most men had a great deal of pride and would do anything to get a job, and accept almost anything in pay: there were no unions in Montgomery, and even if you got a job, there was no assurance it would last—leading some men to take desperate measures.

As a child I recall one such man, "Raymond": A slender man in his late 30s living a hardscrabble life with his wife and nine children in a weather-beaten old house on the edge of town. Unemployed and desperately trying to make ends meet, Ray was walking the street begging employers for a job. With little education and no special skills, he was having no luck. But Ray had hope. It was June and crops were in the field, which meant farmers might need extra help. Also, the canning factory in town started harvesting and canning peas (and soon corn), which meant possible temporary jobs through the canning season.

It happened that Ray came to our meat market for food, offering to do any kind of work to pay for it. Father knew Ray to be conscientious and dependable. Our farm had 30 acres of sweet corn in need of cultivation, and Dad needed help. Ray was hired on a temporary basis for $1.25 per day (not unusual for unskilled labor at that time).

One day, a few weeks after Ray was hired, I was to see how tough the depression was for some men. It was a typical hot and humid June afternoon with no breeze. Father had just finished lunch after spending the morning at the meat market making sausage. He decided to drive out to the farm (just a few blocks from our house) and see how Ray was doing. I jumped in the car to ride along. Ray was supposed to be cultivating corn with the team of horses. As we drove down the narrow gravel road along the cornfield, Dad looked for the swirl of dust thrown up by the horses and cultivator as it went between the rows of corn. But no dust or movement was seen. Then, at the far end of the field sat the cultivator and team—stopped—and no Ray. With alarm, my father jumped out of the car to investigate. Ray was lying in a furrow next to the horses. Was he injured or sick? Dad ran to help. Ray was asleep! Dad shook him awake. "What the hell is going on?" Dad demanded. Ray sheepishly tried to explain.

It seems that a few days before, Ray was offered a temporary night job at the canning factory. Unwilling to turn down the opportunity, he took the job—trying to hold both jobs by working nights at the factory and days on the farm for Dad! Father had to fire Ray.

Some years later I heard Ray had committed suicide. His wife had died, his spirit and will broken, he said he had nothing to live for. So Ray closed the garage door, strung a hose from the car's exhaust to the steering wheel, got in and turned the key...

6.

Why Am I Still Alive?

I WAS BORN, Barton Conrad Bauer, the first of two boys, in the Queen of Peace Hospital in New Prague, Minnesota, the nearest hospital to Montgomery on October 29, 1932. My brother Milton, my only sibling, was born in 1938.

Often I have been asked where I got the Christian name "Barton." No one in town had that name, neither as a first nor last name. It seemed every boy was John, Joe, Jim, Tom, or Albert. For years I thought mother was responsible; just recently she told me Aunt Esther suggested it from Bruce Barton, an advertising executive and writer of popular philosophy of the time. My middle name was for Grandpa Conrad.

But few boys were called by their Christian name; every boy it seemed had a nickname. I was no exception. Mine was "Buck" for Buck Jones, a popular cowboy in B movies in the 1920s, 30s and 40s.

As a boy of five or six I was always running around wearing a cowboy hat, bandanna around my neck, and a cap gun in holster hung low on the hip, playing cowboy and Indians.

I spent the first three years of my life with my mother and father in a four-room apartment in Grandpa Conrad's apartment building called "the flat". It was an unimposing two-story wood-frame structure with galvanized "tin" siding and a tarred flat roof located just off Main Street behind our meat market. There were two apartment units rented out on the second floor, and a chicken hatchery and one apartment unit (where we lived) on the first floor.

My best friend was John (Jack) Kohout. Jack's father owned a harness and shoe shop on Main Street. Jack, his parents and younger brother Jim, lived above the shop, just across the alley from the flat. Farmers brought in the harnesses for their workhorses to be repaired and oiled.

Jack and I loved to play cowboys, our horse being my father's coonhound. Mom told me Jack and I were always talking about going out West to "Mantanna" to be cowboys—and once established coming to get our mothers to take back to live with us.

About 1935, we moved from the flat to live with Grandpa Conrad in his house on the west side of town. My grandfather was in his 70s and living alone. Grandmother Mary had died, my aunts Esther and Dorothy were living and working in the Twin Cities, and Grandpa needed someone to cook and clean for him.

My grandfather had built the house a couple of years after his marriage so they could move out of their apartments above the meat market and have more room when the children started coming.

Grandpa Conrad's two-story white-frame house would seem primitive in today's standards. It was heated with a wood-burning furnace in the basement, and a wood-burning kitchen stove. Water was from a hand pump in the kitchen sink. But Grandpa had made improvements just before we came. He had constructed a toilet and bathtub on the second floor—the outside toilet was gone.

The house had a screened-in front porch with hollyhocks along the east side. In the back was a huge old elm tree with a woodpile against its base. On the west side was an orchard with four apple trees and a garden (potatoes, cabbage, carrots, and onions). About 30 yards behind the house and garden was a narrow gravel road that led to Conrad Bauer and Sons 80-acre farm and "slaughterhouse." Actually the whole farm was referred to as "The Slaughterhouse."

As a kid, I remember a typical day started early. First thing in the morning Grandpa got up and started a fire in the kitchen wood stove. Mom got up a little later and made breakfast. Dad was out of the house soon after, either to the meat market in town or the farm.

My mother was always concerned about my health. My birth was normal (weight 8 lbs., 1 ounce), but Mom says I was a "finicky" eater from the start. At a time when the "healthy" child was fat with rosy cheeks, I had the look of undernourishment about me. "You have to eat more," she would say, "so you can grow up to be big and strong."

And it did not help matters when Mom might hear those subtle hints from some people suggesting deficient mothering, such as: "Why don't you fatten that kid up?" or "Put some meat on his bones!"

When mother expressed concerns to Dad, his impatient response was "Send him out to the wood pile to chop some wood—then he'll get an appetite."

Then there was the fear of colds: Keep out of the draft, always wear a cap, wear overshoes to keep feet warm and dry, and don't go outside with your hair wet were Mom's constant mantras. If I'd get a cough or sniffle she rubbed my chest with Vicks VapoRub, and heated it on the stove so I could breath in its vapors. And an earache meant a hot water bottle pressed against the offending ear after packing it with cotton.

And then the concern about constipation—the fear of getting "bound up." Before the modern emphasis on dietary fiber, constipation was not an uncommon problem. Food tended to be over cooked, to make it soft and "easy on the stomach." Fruits and vegetables were peeled and seldom eaten raw. Consequently, the usual diet was deficient in "roughage." Grandma Holey suffered from recurrent constipation and gave herself enemas to get relief. As a consequence, mother was ever watchful of my regularity, and at the least provocation (up until age four or five) gave me an enema using warm soapy water "to clean me out"—a procedure I never looked forward to.

On the other hand, perhaps mother had reason to be worried about my health. It seems I never missed a childhood disease that came to town, or avoided an accident just waiting to happen.

Mom tells me my first serious illness was convulsions at age three or four. A high fever brought on a seizure: my eyes rolled back, my body shook, and I turned blue. The doctor was called and the crisis passed with no lasting effect.

From convulsions, I ran through the entire directory of childhood infectious diseases: chicken pox, measles, mumps, "yellow jaundice" (hepatitis), and "double pneumonia." To a little boy, yellow jaundice was frightening as my skin and eyes turned yellow: "Ma—is my skin going to stay yellow?" I would ask. To this day I can't donate blood because of having had it.

Pneumonia, when I was a child, was more serious than it is today because antibiotics were not yet available for treatment. Double pneumonia, as the term was then used, meant it was in both lungs. I remember I was in bed for several weeks fighting it.

Later in the 1940s and 1950s the first antibiotic, penicillin, appeared and was considered the "miracle drug" for pneumonia and a host of other infectious diseases. Because of its popularity it may have been over-prescribed. When I went into the Navy in 1952, it was said in some jest that a trip to sick bay for anything from a sore back to a sprained ankle would probably mean a painful shot of penicillin in the buttocks (perhaps more to discourage malingerers than to treat the problem).

Growing up I had my share of accidents: the two most serious before age five. As a toddler, the story goes, I was riding with father in the front seat of the pickup. On a country road approaching a stop sign, the door came open and I toppled out—and narrowly missed being run over by the rear wheels.

The second accident at age four truly was a close call. It was a winter morning (we had recently moved from the flat to Grandpa Conrad's house) and I had been bundled up and sent out to play. Alone and looking for something to do, I wandered across the street to the home of Dr. Otto Vollmar, a veterinarian. Adjacent to his house was a hen house and wire mesh enclosed yard for his laying hens. Being winter the chickens were kept in the hen house, but the gate to the yard was ajar.

Pushing the gate open, I stumbled over a railing about a foot off the ground, and sprawled forearms outstretched across a patch of ice. Embedded in the ice was a broken milk bottle, two large shards of which stood up several inches about the ice. As I fell forward my left forearm slid across the broken glass, opening up two deep gashes (one four inches and the other 1½ inches long) just past my wrist and backward toward the elbow—severing both arteries in my arm.

Perhaps because I was so young, and it was so cold, and the accident happened so fast, I don't remember the pain, but I do remember so vividly watching with casual curiosity as the bright red arterial blood spewed forth in rhythmic spurts—running out my coat sleeve like water from an eave trough.

With enough presence of mind to know the arm needed attention, I went to the Vollmar's house and knocked on the door until Mrs. Pauline Vollmar answered. Having been a school teacher before her marriage, "Paulie" never panicked. She took me in, wrapped a towel tightly around my forearm to stop the bleeding, and called my father at the meat market.

Dad came and took me directly to Dr. Fred Westerman's office on Main Street. "Doc Fred," heavyset with prematurely gray hair and a perpetually unlit cigar in his mouth, tried to ease my fear. Eliciting from father that I wanted to be a cowboy when I grew up, he gently patted my shoulder and said, "You know son, cowboys don't cry"—and I didn't. Even after Dr. Fred started suturing my arm, I held the tears.

I was sent home with a plaster cast covering my arm—and I remember the persistent itch as the wounds healed and not being able to scratch them.

As I grew, the accidents continued: serious cutting of my left forefinger twice (more about that later); and a broken nose, ribs, and front teeth playing football (no face guards or teeth protectors in those days).

But as I look back I don't remember the pain or discomfort of the accidents or the sickness; rather I recall the pleasure of mother's increased attention (as a child) and later (as an adolescent) the chance to read and dream.

My earliest memory as a little boy is mother rocking me in Grandpa Conrad's old wooden rocking chair next to the wood stove. If I wasn't feeling well, or just restless before bedtime, she would motion me to her lap, rock gently and sing softly: "We'll build a sweet little nest … somewhere in the West … and let the rest of the world go by."

After I cut my arm and through the days of healing, there was Mom every day reading to me those exotic stories from a Bible picture book: David and Goliath, the Good Samaritan, the Prodigal Son …

As I got older, the mumps, hepatitis, and pneumonia afforded me a week or more away from school and allowed me the solitude of the sick room—time to read comic books (*Batman and Robin*, my favorite), and later Big-Little Books (*Red Ryder*), and adventure magazines (TRUE and ARGOSY).

As I grew into adulthood my chief escape became books, and to a lesser degree movies. My favorite authors were short story writers, such as Guy de Maupassant and O Henry; and particularly those whose settings were exotic: W. Somerset Maugham and James Michener (Pacific Islands and Southeast Asia) and Jack London (Alaska)—they wrote about places where only my imagination could take me.

Maugham, to this day, holds particular fascination. About every ten years I reread most of his short stories—one of which ("Red") has given me much thought of late because of my own experiences as a young sailor in the Philippine Islands.

Actually reading can become something of an addiction—something a person must do every day. W. Somerset Maugham in his short story, "The Book-Bag," describes this habit well. Maugham would become anxious and irritable if caught without reading material for any length of time. When going on a journey, he would pack a huge sack "to the brim with books to suit every possible occasion and mood." To him reading was a drug he could not do without.

I must confess to the same affliction. I rarely go anywhere without taking a book or two. When my wife Shirley, the children, and I went to Lake Mille Lacs in Northern Minnesota on one or two weeks vacation, I would go to the library and pack a shopping bag full of books to carry me through. I am drawn like a junkie to the neighborhood library or Barnes & Noble Booksellers to browse at least three times a week.

Shirley tells me I am totally indifferent to the house, with the exception of the den—my reading room—where the "easy" chair and reading lamp have to be just so.

And just the thought of books and the solitude of a reading room can affect me like a drug. Before retirement, I can remember times of high job stress when I suffered from insomnia. To help me fall asleep, I would imagine going deep in an underground cavern, walking through darkened stairways and secret doors into a windowless room with walls lined with books and a cushioned reclining chair and reading lamp.

I would be alone—no one would know my whereabouts. Depending on my mood, there might be soft background music: something like Claude Thornhill's "Snowfall" or Debussy's "Clair de Lune." I would slowly browse through the shelves of books, select one and settle into the recliner. Invariably before I opened the book, sleep would come.

Rose Bauer, my mother, reading to me. I have always loved books. Maybe this is where it started.

Left: Bart, 3 years old

Below: Grandpa Conrad Bauer on his easy chair in the parlor of our home on 502 Oak Ave. W. It is Easter time, about 1940. My brother Milt is in grandpa's lap. I am the one on the right with the patched trousers.

Left: Here I am (with cap gun, holster, bandana around my neck, and straw hat) playing cowboy. I got my nickname "Buck" from the silent film star of the day, Buck Jones.

My cousin Mary Bauer and I as pioneers with a covered wagon and two live oxen, posing behind Grandpa's house. I'm holding Grandpa Conrad's double barrel shotgun and Mary her baby (her doll). We were representing Bauer's Pioneer Meat Market in the Kolacky Day parade (1939 or 1940).

Confirmed on April 14, 1946 (age 13) at St. John Lutheran Church in Montgomery, MN by Rev. Conrad J. Buehler. I am in the front row, second from the left.

Mom, Dad, Milt and I behind our house at 502 Oak Ave. W. just before our 6-week trip through the western states, June to July 1947 (I was 14 and Milt was 9)

III. THE SPORTING LIFE

7.

Guns, Traps and Fish Poles

HUNTING, TRAPPING AND FISHING were my life growing up. Whenever my father and Grandpa Jim, Mom's father, got together, the talk was hunting. They knew nothing about football and basketball, and little about baseball—and cared less. Uncle Bill, along with hunting, loved fishing and bought fur from local trappers.

So it was not unusual that I got my first gun just before my sixth birthday: a silver-barreled Daisy BB gun.

And Dad and Grandpa Conrad soon gave me a job: shooting the blackbirds that flocked in our sweet corn field and ate the corn. I never hit many, but I scared the dickens out of them.

But sparrows were easy targets. In late summer evenings they would bunch up on certain trees, noisy and quarrelsome and indifferent to our presence.

Our neighbor, Ray Wondra, had a small tree hanging over his chicken coop. For several weeks every year the sparrows would cluster in that tree, soiling the coop with their droppings. Ray welcomed BB guns, and watched with pleasure as my friends and I shot one sparrow after another out of the tree. I would shoot 15 or 20 every evening, fill a large paper bag with dead sparrows, and take them to the farm to feed our cats: a win-win situation all around—except for the sparrows.

After supper one evening when I was nine years old, my father pushed his plate aside and said, "It's time you had a .22."

For Dad, having a .22-caliber rifle was as necessary as having clothes to wear or his cigarettes. He always kept a .22 under the front seat of his car for shooting pheasants along the road during his trips to farms to buy cattle. For him, knowing how to handle a rifle and hunt game was a necessary rite of passage for a boy.

The next morning we went to David's Jewelry Store (across the street from our meat market) where old Matt David handled a line of firearms as well as the usual jewelry, watches (and watch repair), and other gift items.

The little bell above the door jingled as Dad and I came in. Matt removed the optical lens from his eye and pushed up from the table where he had been repairing a watch.

"We're looking for a .22 rifle for the boy," Dad said, nodding to me as we moved to the counter with a line of rifles and shotguns against the wall.

Matt showed us the .22s so Dad and I could handle the guns.

Two I particularly liked. I threw each in turn to my shoulder, sighting in along the barrel at Matt's big grandfather clock at the far end of the store. "This one handles best for me, Pa," I said, handing him a Remington bold action "Targetmaster." The price tag was about ten dollars and change.

"It's yours, Bart," Dad said, adding a box of .22 "short" cartridges to the deal. I left David's store walking mighty tall.

My first "kill" came a few days later.

The pasture on Grandpa Conrad's farm had a small grove of hardwood trees. The farmer next to Grandpa's had a line fence that came to a "T" in the woods: a corner of which held a huge brush pile of rusted barb wire, old tree stumps and branches, rocks, and weeds—a haven for cottontails.

It was after supper on a warm, early fall evening that I took the .22 and walked the half mile to the tree line. I got to the brush pile about an hour or so before dusk, when rabbits come out to feed, and took a position behind a big elm tree about 30 feet from the brush pile, then hunkered down and waited.

It wasn't long before a cottontail hopped out into full view, then crouched down, eyes and ears alert to danger. As I moved slightly to get into firing position, the rabbit's ears stood up, waving backward and forward—it heard me.

I waited, then slowly raised the rifle and tried to aim at the rabbit's head. But I was so nervous my body started trembling, the rifle wavered—I had buck fever. For a minute or so I just took deep breaths until my arms steadied, then sighted in and shot. The rabbit jumped straight in the air and dropped—dead—a clean kill!

I was so excited I ran home to show Mom and Dad, then into the basement to skin and gut the rabbit. Dad had a rule that whomever brought home game had to clean it so Mom could cook it. When I finished, Mom washed the meat. Next day she pan-fried the rabbit in butter, added onions, pepper and salt—and we had it for supper. It was a big day for me—now I was a hunter.

My favorite rabbit hunting territory was along the railroad tracks that formed the southern boundary of our farm. One side of the tracks was grown up in weeds. The soil was mostly peat, spongy and dark-colored, and littered with underground rabbit burrows. About dusk in winter I would walk the tracks, and with my .22 in hand, watch for rabbits hunched up in the snow just outside their burrows. It was important that the first shot was a kill, as a wounded rabbit crawled back into its burrow and was lost. It was not unusual for me to get one or two rabbits each evening. As I got older, I liked to hunt squirrels (both Fox and Gray) with my dog, King, a mixed-breed hound and Airedale Terrier. When I was old enough to drive a car, I would take King into the country on an autumn afternoon and look for a cornfield next to woods. Squirrels liked corn, and would leave their "den trees" (where the squirrel had its nest inside the tree trunk) and travel some distance to the cornfield to feed.

I would turn King loose in the cornfield to roust any squirrels and give chase. Before a squirrel could get back to the hole in its den tree and escape, King would "tree" the squirrel on a tree close to the cornfield—exposed and easy to shoot.

My best hunting day was when King chased six fox squirrels into two small trees. I shot each in the head (so the meat was not damaged), one after the other. After cleaning, Mom made Vomacka (a Czech sour cream soup) that included with the squirrel meat potatoes, onions, cream, bay leaves, vinegar, salt, and pepper.

When I got big enough to handle a shotgun (about 14 years old), I started hunting pheasants and ducks with an old 16-guage shotgun. But I had trouble right from the start: I couldn't hit birds "on the wing."

I would use King to flush pheasants into the air for me, but my shot missed more often than not. Seeing the pheasant fly off after the shotgun's blast was as disappointing to King, I think, as it was to me. I had the same trouble shooting ducks. I just never got the knack of hitting birds in flight.

Starting about age nine, and for the next few years, I tried my hand at trapping weasels. It was a wintertime activity and a way of making a few dollars.

The weasel is one of the toughest little fighters on four legs. With a body length of 6 or 10 inches, and never more than a few ounces in weight, the weasel has been known to attack animals as large as a horse.

Weasels like the taste of fresh blood, sucked from the neck or base of the skull of the victims they kill. Most of their fare is made up of mice, birds, rats, and rabbits. They like to kill just for the thrill of killing—and there are records of a single weasel getting into a hen house and killing as many as 40 chickens in a single night.

Weasels hunt mostly at night. They have good eyesight, a keen sense of smell, and a built-in curiosity that causes them to investigate any scent trail that their nose encounters.

Weasels are brown during the summer, but turn white in winter with a tiny black tip on their tail. Known to the fur trade as ermine, the prime winter pelts are the only ones that have any value.

Although their fur did not pay much, weasels were rather easy to trap, as they have no fear of man or traps—and, for me, were close at hand. Running through our farm, and next to the woods, was a county drainage ditch with a stream of water about two or three feet deep, and with weeds and brush along its banks—a natural haven for mice, rats, rabbits, and birds—a happy hunting ground for weasels.

With the start of winter and snow on the ground, I would set up a trap line along the ditch and fence line. On a weekend after the first snow, I headed out—loaded down with a small sack containing six or eight steel spring leg-hold traps, several wooden stakes, a can of bloody rabbit liver and entrails, a small hatchet in a leather belt sheath hanging from my waist, and a sharp pocketknife—and looked for weasel tracks in the snow.

If I found evidence of weasel activity, I would set a trap at the bottom of a fence post or tree, or stake the trap near the water along the ditch, then tie a thumb-size chunk of rabbit liver and gut to the trigger. When the weasel tried to take the bait, the trap would snap shut, holding the weasel by the body. In most cases, the trap killed the weasel quickly. In this way, I set all the traps before returning home.

Then I established a routine. On the weekend or after school, I walked the trap line checking each trap. Those traps with weasels were reset with fresh bait; other traps were sometimes moved to better locations or got additional bait.

Returning from the trap line, I skinned the weasels in the basement, and stretched each over a wooden drying board. After a day or two of drying, I combed and brushed out the pelts.

Next came selling the weasel pelts. Although there were other fur buyers, I only sold to Uncle Bill. The going rate was between 25 cents and a dollar, depending on the size and condition of the pelt.

When I went into high school, I quit trapping. My father needed me to help in the shop after school, and I never made enough money trapping to make it worthwhile.

In 1997, after Dad died and Mom went into a nursing home, my brother Milt and I and our wives were cleaning out our parents' home in preparation for sale. In the attic I found an old journal of Uncle Bill's showing his fur-buying activity for the fall and winter of 1943–44.

Uncle Bill's journal gave interesting information about a small-town fur buyer's business. There was a separate section for each animal whose fur he purchased: fox, mink, muskrat, raccoon, skunk, weasel, and civet cat (a small spotted skunk). In each section, Bill listed the name of the person he purchased pelts from, the date, and price paid. Then he noted the name of the buyer he, in turn, sold the pelts to (Joe Wishy in Minneapolis was a frequent name), the price received, and his net profit.

Over 300 trappers and hunters from Le Sueur and Rice counties sold fur to Uncle Bill during that trapping season. Some trappers were big producers—examples: On December 3 and 4, 1943, Albert David of Montgomery sold Uncle Bill 318 muskrat pelts for $572.40. For the season, John Trzecinski, Sr. and his son, John Trzecinski, Jr., of Le Center sold Bill the following skins: mink—10 for $136; muskrats—304 for $482.25; and raccoon—two for $15. Others might sell Bill only one or two pelts all year.

Uncle Bill's journal summarized his fur-buying activity for the year:

Total Pelts Purchased	7,868
Total Purchase Price of All Pelts	$15,495.14
Total Sale Price of All Pelts	$17,046.30
Net Profit for Season 1943-44	$1,1551.16

The ultimate destination of the 7,868 pelts Uncle Bill handled was, of course, the fur-apparel manufacturers located in such cities as New York and St. Louis. Fur coats were prized both for their warmth and for their beauty—and reflected the wearer's financial status. Animal rights groups had not yet made their appearance.

How attitudes have changed. After Aunt Esther died in 1993, Aunt Dorothy gave Esther's mink fur coat to my wife, Shirley. It was a beautiful garment, but had not been worn for years and was in need of repair. Shirley spent $135 to have the coat relined and cleaned, yet she has never worn it. Fur coats are so out of fashion now that to wear one in public is to invite nasty comments—or worse.

My father was not a fur buyer like Uncle Bill, but he did trap. However, his trapping was completely different: He trapped animals for their meat, not their fur. He used homemade box traps, not steel leg-hold traps. He first started trapping after his retirement and continued into his late 80s. And Dad never went more than 40 feet from the back door of his house to set his traps. How was this you might ask?

Well, Mom and Dad liked squirrel and rabbit meat. But it was hard work tramping the woods and fields to hunt them. And besides, there were more squirrels and rabbits in town and around my parents' house than in the country. There was more food, and fewer predators to kill them. More people had bird feeders, and even fed squirrels and rabbits. And you could not shoot them in town.

So my father built box traps out of wood and wire to catch his meal. His box traps had a drop-type sliding door attached by a string to a trigger. He attached a cob of corn to the trigger. When a squirrel or rabbit went into the box and began eating the corn, the trigger was forced out of a notch, and the door dropped down behind it.

In the fall and early winter, Dad put his box trap near several apple trees in his backyard. For weeks he put corn near the box trap to feed the squirrels and rabbits—getting them familiar with the box as well as getting them fat.

Dad could watch the activity from a bedroom window. When the time was right, he put the corn in the box and set it. Squirrels, in particular, went right in and were caught. It was as simple as that.

For years, Mom and Dad had all the squirrel and rabbit they wanted. What they didn't eat fresh, they froze for eating the rest of the year.

Dad was even called upon to take his box trap to Aunt Esther and Dorothy's house in St. Paul, to clean out squirrels digging up their garden. These too went into my parents' larder.

Fishing and swimming were important summertime activities for kids, and it was easy and cost little. Lakes were within biking distance, and all you needed to fish was a cane pole, hook, line, sinker, bobber—and a can of worms. Since there were no public swimming pools in town, our swimming was done in the same lakes in which we fished.

As I write, I am looking at an old picture. It shows some friends and I getting ready to go fishing. We are on bikes—cane poles tied on, with a gunnysack to hold any fish caught.

Our destination most likely was Greenleaf Lake, about three miles south of Montgomery; or the Cannon River that flows under Highway 13 six miles south of town. Most fish caught were bullheads and an occasional sunfish or crappie. All fish caught were taken home, cleaned and given to our Moms for frying.

My fishing days as a kid bring to mind a poignant memory about a misadventure and the loss of a friend.

I first met Chuck H. when we started sixth grade together in the fall of 1942. Chuck, his younger brother Bob, and his parents had moved to Montgomery that summer from a small town on the Iowa border. Chuck's Dad worked for the M & St. L Railroad as a part of a section crew responsible for railroad track maintenance.

Chuck, a good-looking boy with light brown hair and slender build, sat across from me in class. He was a prankster; always teasing the girls, especially the girl that sat in front of him—threatening to dip her pigtail in his inkwell. He created excitement, and I was drawn to him.

The following summer in 1943, Chuck, Bob, and I spent much time fishing, swimming, and just hanging out. One morning Chuck suggested we hitchhike—rather than bike—to the Cannon River to fish. We had never hitchhiked before, but we thought, Why not? We took fishing gear, packed sandwiches and lemonade, and, along with Chuck's dog, a black and white mixed breed Collie, we started walking—with thumbs up—heading south on Highway 13.

It wasn't long before a battered pickup truck with two middle-aged men in bib overalls pulled up.

"Where you kids headed?" the burly driver asked.

"Cannon River—we're going fishing," said Chuck.

"That's where we're going. Hop in the back," said the driver, jerking his thumb back toward the truck's open box. "We'll take you there."

We piled in the truck box, dog and all; and with the wind in our hair and the noise from the truck's worn-out muffler and loose fenders roaring in our ears—held on tight as the truck sped off.

We were excited, what a way to go—a lot easier and more fun than biking out. But when we got to the river, the truck did not stop, it barreled past. Bewildered at first, then frantic, we pounded on the cab and shouted out; the truck went on.

About 15 minutes later, the truck pulled into the town of Waterville, 16 miles south of Montgomery, and stopped at a picnic area where the Cannon River meandered by. "Here you go boys," said the driver. "Good luck fishing."

We tried to explain we wanted off where the river crossed the highway, and asked why he didn't stop when we hollered.

"Sorry boys," said the driver. "I thought you wanted to fish the river here. Sure we heard you all bouncing around in the back, but just thought you were having some fun."

"Will you take us back?" asked Chuck.

"Nope," said the driver. "I don't have time. Why don't you boys fish awhile. You'll find a way back home."

Too young to argue, we got out and went to a picnic table near the river. What to do now? We were a long way from home. And except for a few cents in our pockets, were broke. I had never been to Waterville and was not sure about trying to hitchhike back to Montgomery. As fear took hold, I lost interest in fishing.

Then Chuck, ever the optimist and looking at our predicament as an adventure, came up with a solution. "We can walk back," he assured us. "My Dad took me here on a railroad handcar all the way from Montgomery once. The tracks are over there." He pointed to a tree line several blocks away. "All we have to do is start walking north—it'll take us right home."

So without better ideas, we ate our lunch and, just before noon, started walking the railroad tracks, not fully realizing what we were in for.

But soon Chuck had us laughing and joking, telling stories as we walked along, throwing rocks at telephone poles—turning the whole situation into a lark. Even the dog (I can't remember its name) got into the act: big time.

It was late in the afternoon when the Collie's frenzied barking had us running to a pile of railroad cross ties and brush. There was an animal in there somewhere, and the dog was after it. On our approach, the Collie, emboldened by our presence, crawled halfway into the pile—and paid the price.

The animal was a skunk, and the Collie got a spray of the biting, evil-smelling liquid right in the face. Out came the dog, shaking its head, rubbing its eyes against its leg, and frothing from the mouth.

Even Chuck, who got to the pile ahead of us, got part of the salvo from the skunk's scent gland. Of course, Bob and I got a laugh out of that.

However, by this time we had been walking six hours and getting tired and worried. But Chuck, ever confident, sustained our spirits by pointing out landmarks: a creek here, an unusual barn there that he recognized from his handcar journey with his Dad.

Then in the distance, just as it was getting dark, we recognized the nightlights of the Minnesota Valley canning factory. We were home!

We were a bedraggled bunch—tired, dirty, hungry, and smelling to high heaven—as we walked the short distance from the railroad tracks to my house. We noticed Chuck's parents' car outside.

It seems when we did not return for supper, our parents got together, and worried, tried to figure out what to do. They were angry when we first walked in, then, after hearing our story, relieved we were safe. Our judgment in the situation was not seriously questioned.

But the story ends on a sad note. It wasn't too long after our misadventure that Chuck's mother, a pretty lady with black hair, got involved with a guard at the prisoner of war camp next to the canning factory. Chuck's parents separated, and the father took the boys and moved to LeRoy, Minnesota. I never heard from Chuck or Bob again.

I remember I missed Chuck a great deal, and thought of him often. We were best buddies, and the separation was akin to a teenage boy leaving his girl friend, going into the army, and never hearing from her again. I guess the bonding of 12-year-old boys can be as intense, until the emergence of puberty turns their attention to girls.

Some years later, I heard Chuck had worked as a truck driver and later died from a heart attack.

8.

Man's Best Friend

SOMETIME AFTER MY father's death in 1994, mother asked me to look through Dad's clothes and personal effects to determine, with my brother Milt, what should be kept and what should be given away to relatives, friends, or some charity. Since everything Dad cherished most was kept in his bedroom (in later years Mom and Dad had separate bedrooms) that is where I looked first.

My father's bedroom was plainly furnished: a bed, dresser, clothes closet, chair—and two chests Mom used to store blankets and old tax records. But prominent in one corner was Dad's glass-framed gun cabinet with his guns (a .257 Roberts "deer rifle," a Winchester 12-guage shotgun, and a Winchester .22-caliber rifle) proudly displayed. And in the top drawer of his dresser were two timeworn photograph albums, and a small blue book.

The albums were filled with photos of my father and his dogs: from the 1920s, when he was a young man, until the last few years of his life. Many pictures showed Dad proudly holding a raccoon or fox he had shot.

The name of the book was *The Coonhound* by Robert Legare, published in 1924 by the Hunter-Trader-Trapper Co. of Columbus, Ohio. It was described as a practical treatise on the origin, breeding, training, care, and hunting of the coonhound. In the inside cover and blank pages of the book, my father had written the names and birth dates of his coonhounds born between July 15, 1936 and April 11, 1973. On one page of the book, just before the title page, was a picture of a coonhound beneath which in capital letters, were the words by Byron:

BEAUTY, WITHOUT VANITY,
STRENGTH WITHOUT INSOLENCE
COURAGE WITHOUT FEROCITY,
AND ALL THE VIRTUES OF MAN
WITHOUT HIS VICES

The albums and book remind me today of how important dogs were to my father, and how big a part they played in my childhood.

In the 1930s and 40s, my father maintained a pack of coonhounds at the Slaughterhouse farm. Usually the pack included two experienced older hounds, several young hounds, and, sometimes, a bitch (female) with puppies. The older dogs each had their own doghouse; the younger ones and the bitch and puppies were kept in a wire-enclosed kennel attached to the chicken house.

My father fed the coonhounds horsemeat. When farmers started replacing their work horses with tractors, my father bought horses cheap. In the winter we butchered horses, and hung quarters of horse carcass in the hide house. I remember chopping off chunks of frozen horsemeat to feed the dogs.

The meat we fed the hounds was lean, and together with beef bones to chew and exercise, kept the dogs in good condition. Dad could hunt the coonhounds until they were about 12 or 13 years old: that's when their hearing and eyesight started to fail. With cold Minnesota winters and the hounds in outdoor doghouses, I cannot recall a hound living beyond 14 years of age.

My father's coonhounds were not purebred, they carried no pedigree "papers." Some were of the "Bluetick" breed, others were "Redbone," and still others were "Black and Tan." Yet his best dog for coon hunting was "Coke"—a "Walker" foxhound. In fact all his hounds would hunt coon or fox, whichever Dad was hunting at the time. Also, some were open trailers and others were silent trailers—that is they did not bark on trail, only when they had treed the coon.

The key to success as a coon hunter was to have a good coonhound. To get a good coonhound, one had to start with a pup whose parents were proven coon dogs.

In a small town most hunters knew one another and knew who had the best coon dogs. To get promising pups, one hunter might agree to breed his stud dog to another hunter's bitch and both share the pups. For years, my father had an excellent stud dog, Coke, and other hunters brought their female dogs to be bred by him. For this service, Dad might take a pick of the litter of puppies.

My father was very pragmatic in selecting and training his coon dogs. If he had a bitch with a litter of pups, he took only the healthy and active ones. The unwanted pups were put in a gunnysack and drowned in the cement stock tank.

When the pups were old enough to hunt, Dad trained each by hunting the youngster with an old experienced coonhound. If the young dog showed no promise, or could not be broken of bad habits, such as running rabbits, fighting the other hunting dogs, or was "gun shy" (would run in fear at the sound of gun fire)—my father would shoot the young dog.

To Dad's way of thinking, if a hunting dog could not perform adequately, it was of no use. Hound dogs were not "house dogs" or pets; they were bred and trained to hunt. My father would not sell, or even give away, any hunting dog that did not hunt. Yes, he had feelings about destroying a young hound—it was not something he enjoyed doing—but he felt it had to be done.

Actually, drowning pups or shooting old or unwanted dogs was not seen as a cruelty: at least not in a farm community in those days. There were no animal shelters as there are today, and I don't recall hunters taking unwanted dogs to a veterinarian to be "put to sleep." An experience of mine might illustrate this attitude.

It was a pleasant Sunday afternoon in late fall—and Indian summer day—when, with my father, we drove out to a farm west of town. The farmer, George H., had a bull to sell: a routine cattle-buying visit for Dad. I was about 11 years old.

After the bargaining was done and the sale completed, Dad and George leaned against the fence next to the cattle barn and visited. George knew my father was a coon hunter, and soon the talk turned to dogs. Although George wasn't a hunter, he had several farm collies and was concerned about one: an old cattle dog he'd had for years who now was deaf and almost blind. He kept the Collie outdoors in a doghouse and did not think the dog could survive the cold winter. He thought the dog should be put down, but didn't have the heart to shoot it.

My father tipped his hat back and said softly, "We can help you on that score, George. My boy can shoot the dog for you."

The farmer gave me a quizzical look, but after my father's reassurance, agreed.

My father told me to get his .22 from under the car seat and asked George to bring the old Collie. After I got the .22 we watched as the farmer, head down, walked slowly to the farmhouse where the old Collie was lying in the sun next to the doghouse. There he cut a six foot length of "binder" twine to make a leash, and looped one end loosely around the dog's neck. He knelt next to the Collie and, for several minutes, gently patted the dog's head and side, whispering softly in ears that did not hear. The Collie, tail wagging, nestled his head against the farmer's chest.

Dad checked the .22 to make sure it was loaded and the safety on, then handed the rifle to me. He nodded at the farmer and his dog and said, "That old dog has served his master well. He deserves to die quick and clean—no pain. You take the dog in the woods behind those big elms so George don't see you shoot him—and in the head—then come back—leave the dog lay."

The old Collie was gaunt and unsteady on its legs as it followed the farmer to the barn where Dad and I waited. With a nod from my father, I took the leash from the farmer and, with the Collie following docilely at my heels, walked slowly down the cattle lane to the grove of trees.

I took the old Collie behind a big elm tree out of sight from the farm buildings. When the dog knew I was going no further, he lay down, head on his front paws, and dozed in the sun's warmth. I went to pet him, but held back: it did not seem right for what I was going to do.

For several minutes I watched as the Collie's breathing slowed, his eyes closed—then I put the rifle to his head and squeezed the trigger. The dog's body jerked, stiffened, and was still.

Later in the car going home, I did not feel much like talking. My feelings were confused. I did as I was told, and I did it right, but I didn't feel good.

When I was growing up, coon hunting was my father's passion. I can remember the excitement each night when Dad and Grandpa Jim, also a coon hunter, loaded the hounds in the car and headed to their favorite woods to hunt. They each took an experienced coonhound and often a young dog to train. Most often the hunt did not end until well after midnight. Because I had school the next day, I was able to go along only on occasion during weekends.

The raccoon is classified as a medium-sized mammal with the average adult weight of 12 to 16 pounds. (The largest raccoon Dad ever bagged weighed 32 pounds). Two well-known features are its black "burglar" mask over its eyes and its bushy ringed tail. Raccoon are very intelligent, and it has been said are much smarter than cats or rats, but not quite up to monkeys.

In the North, raccoons breed during January and February and have young in March and April. There are usually 3 to 5 babies in a litter. The normal life span of a raccoon is from 10 to 12 years.

When it comes to eating, raccoons will eat just about anything. In late spring and early summer, the bulk of its food is composed of animals such as crayfish, earthworms, slugs, frogs, turtles and their eggs, snails, insects, young rabbits or young muskrats. In late summer and fall they feed more often on vegetable matter such as berries, acorns, garden vegetables—and especially corn when it is just ripe.

Raccoon are active and feed at night. During autumn, they embark in an orgy of eating and accumulate a layer of body fat that sustains them throughout the cold winter months.

As you can see from the raccoon's diet, when my father and Grandpa Jim went coon hunting, they looked for a wooded area near a cornfield, river, or lake. After finding a suitable spot, they parked the car, turned the hounds loose, lowered the windows, then waited—and listened.

Except for Coke, the hounds were open trailers. And once an open trailer scents a raccoon, he bays every few steps on the trail. The fresher the trail, the more excited the dog becomes and the more noise he makes. Dad and Grandpa Jim loved the sound of the hunt, and could tell just what each dog was doing by the particular bark, bay, bellow, or yelp the dog gave tongue to.

When the raccoon hears the dogs barking, it tries to escape. If young, or a novice in being hunted, the raccoon will crawl up the nearest tree. Grandpa Jim and Dad could tell from the sound of the hounds' barks when they had a raccoon treed. Then it was just a matter of walking to the sound of the dogs and shooting the raccoon out of the tree.

However, it becomes more difficult if the raccoon has been hunted before, and knows how to fool the hounds. The racoon may run until it reaches a hollow den tree and escape inside. Or it may run along the tops of rail fences, or leave a maze of tracks to confuse the dogs. Or take to water to escape.

A raccoon in water can be deadly to a dog. If the racoon can find a floating log or branch, it climbs up on it and then, reaching out, holds the pursuing dog's head underwater. If a dog catches up to a swimming raccoon in open water, the raccoon climbs right up on the dog's head and submerges it.

And a raccoon is not only wily, but a tough street fighter. It is strong and if cornered, will fight viciously. Most coonhounds have shredded ears and faces covered with scars to prove it. Some say that pound for pound, an adult raccoon can beat almost any dog going.

Sometimes an old "buck coon," weighing as much as 30 pounds, will get a reputation as being too smart and tough for the hounds to handle. As soon as he hears the dogs bark on his trail, he uses all his tricks and escapes. If, by chance, he is caught by the dogs, he manages to fight them off and still get away.

When my father went after one of these crafty old-timers, he took just Coke. Coke was fast and did not bark on trail. Before the old coon knew he was being hunted, Coke was on him. And he did not try to kill the coon. He seemed to know that in a death struggle, he would not come out unscathed. Coke tried to hold the coon on the ground—barking, circling, darting in and out like a counter punching boxer; biting at the coon's haunches when he tried to escape to a den tree or to water—until Dad came and shot the coon.

My father never got tired of talking about Coke. I know more about that dog than I do about some of our relatives.

Dad kept a 7x9-inch framed picture of Coke hanging on the wall at home. His albums contain a dozen pictures of Coke in various poses over the dog's lifetime.

A beautiful dog of the Foxhound (American) breed, Coke was solid white in color with a six-inch black spot on his right side, and black ears and black markings around his eyes. In his little blue book, *The Coonhound*, my father penciled in Coke's birth date: "St. Peter Coke—Sept. 20, 1937."

Dad told the story of how he got Coke. In 1938, he was looking for a coonhound and heard of two brothers near St. Peter, Minnesota who farmed and raised hunting dogs for sale. The farm, he said, was a menagerie of dogs of every description, but the coonhounds for sale were priced too high. Then, almost as an afterthought, one of the dog-dealer brothers mentioned he had a year old foxhound he would sell cheap.

The young hound was chained to a corncrib, and when the dog dealer and my father approached, crawled under the corncrib and would not come out. Angry, the dealer grabbed the chain and, hand over hand, dragged the dog out. Once out, the dog stood trembling, tail between his legs, head bowed, in front of his master.

The dog was in bad condition: patches of his hair were missing, the skin beneath red, thickened and wrinkled from mange; the body undernourished, the backbone prominent, the flanks sunken, a bony ridge along the right side suggested healed over broken ribs.

The dealer, anticipating my father's questions, said, "I'll be square with you. I've had trouble with this hound. He chased chickens on me, bothered my laying hens. I whipped him good for it, and gave him a boot in the ribs for good measure. He don't bother chickens now." He went on to say that the dog was a loner and did not join in with the other dogs in killing a coon—just was not a fighter. To this dealer, serious shortcomings in a coonhound.

The thinking that a good coonhound should be a good coon fighter and killer was not unusual. For some old-time coon hunters, half the fun was watching the hounds kill a raccoon. Instead of shooting the raccoon, they would climb the tree and poke or push the raccoon from its perch with a stick. Then they would watch the dogs try to kill the raccoon on the ground.

These fights were always stacked heavily in favor of the dogs because the average hound outweighed the average raccoon by about three to one. The dogs tried to work in pairs so that one could grab the raccoon from the rear and throw it off balance while the other dog grabbed the raccoon's throat or chest for a killing bite. To circumvent an attack like this, the raccoon usually backed up against a rock or tree so all the dogs had to come in from the front. Sometimes the raccoon rolled on its back to fight so as to bring its sharp claws, as well as its teeth, into play—in the same fashion that bobcats fight.

To gradually make a fighter and killer out of a young coonhound, various methods were used. Some old-time trainers advise "blooding" a young dog: by ripping the coon open and smearing the dog's chest, throat, and forelegs with blood as soon as the coon is killed. However, others thought it better to simply feed the dog some of the raw coon meat.

My father did not think it important that a good coonhound be a fighter. He would never think of poking a raccoon out of a tree just to watch the dogs try to kill it. He wanted the coonhound to either tree the raccoon, or hold it on the ground until he could come and shoot it. And he had good reasons:

First, there was too much danger his dogs would get injured: lose an eye or have a nose ripped open in the fight.

Second, Dad did not want the raccoon's pelt torn up. His pelts were in prime condition when sold and brought "top dollar": about $10 each. In his best year of coon hunting, my father got 72 raccoons for a total of about $700—more than a year's salary for some working men.

Finally, my father did not want the raccoon carcass damaged. Some people liked raccoon meat. Every year Dad donated raccoon carcasses to the Faribault or Montgomery VFW for its annual coon feed. And sometimes we had a raccoon dinner. Dad would carefully peel off every bit of fat from the carcass and Mom would roast it. Our hired man, Fred, liked roasted raccoon so much that he would eat the cold leftovers for breakfast the next day.

No, my father wanted a smart dog, not a fighter, and in this young foxhound—named Coke by the dealer—he saw the possibility. Besides, the dealer would settle for $5 for the dog—not an expensive risk to take.

My father bought Coke, and in the days that followed, took pains to gentle the dog. He treated the mange with a mixture that included turpentine, linseed oil, and kerosene—and finally cured it. And he added cow's milk and bread to Coke's diet of raw meat to strengthen him.

As it turned out, Coke became an outstanding coonhound. Other coon hunters wanted to buy him. Uncle Bill offered Dad $5 a pound for Coke. For fun, my father put Coke on a scale and he weighed out at 60 pounds—$300 would have been a princely sum for a coonhound. But Dad maintained, "No money will buy Coke, and no other man will hunt him."

And I don't think another man could hunt Coke. He was "a one man dog". My father told this story: When he shot a coon off the tree and Grandpa Jim went to pick it up, Coke leaned against Grandpa's leg—tried to push him away—so Dad would take the coon instead. Coke hunted for my father—only.

As Coke's fame spread throughout the area, coon hunters brought their female hounds to our farm for Coke to breed. My father would take Coke and the bitch into an upstairs room in the old house, close the door on the two dogs, then go about doing chores. In answer to my inquiries, he said, "Coke will let us know when he's finished his business." And he did.

The window on the upstairs room was covered with a tin sheet with one corner pulled up. When Coke finished "his business", he stuck his head out the opening and rattled the tin to let us know his job was done, and he wanted out.

When Coke turned 14 years old, he lost his hearing and was too frail to hunt. With winter coming, Dad moved Coke and his doghouse into our garage and close to a potbellied wood stove for warmth. But old age caught up to Coke, and several months later he died.

Coke continued to serve even after death. His legacy to my father was two sons, Jack and Blue—both excellent coonhounds Dad hunted for the next 10 years.

9.

For the Love of a Dog

MY FATHER WAS not one to show feelings. I never saw him cry. But he was capable of intense emotion, as made clear in four stories he told of personal anguish. One such incident, of course, was when he had to tell Uncle Bill he would not recover from cancer. The other three, however, involved dogs, and occurred over a span of 50 years.

The first painful situation about a dog happened when Dad was in his early 20s. He had a huge. brown, mixed-breed male mastiff he called "Butso". The two were inseparable. One day my father was hauling the carcass of a butchered steer into town to the meat market. Butso, as usual, was running ahead of the truck, leading the way and providing "protection". Just as Dad pulled into the alley, behind the meat market and Kohout's Harness Shop, Mike Kohout's little terrier ran out barking. Butso saw this as a challenge, locked jaws on the little dog, shook it as if it were a rag doll, and left it badly injured.

Mike Kohout was angry and confronted Grandpa Conrad in the meat market. He explained what happened and said Butso was a menace, not only to other pets, but to children as well. He warned that if Butso hurt a child, Grandpa Conrad and his business could be sued.

Mike's words hit home. Grandpa Conrad's business was his life and any threat needed immediate action. Grandfather promised Mike that Butso would not bother him again.

Grandpa Conrad was angry. He was not a hunter, never had a dog, and did not like Butso. There had been problems with the dog before, and this was the last straw. He went to the back room where Dad was unloading the truck. "That damn dog is no good," he shouted, pointing his finger at Butso. "He causes trouble for me." He turned to Dad and said, "I don't want to see that dog again. Take him out to the Slaughterhouse and shoot him."

My father was stunned. He protested, but to no avail. Grandpa Conrad's word was final; there was no "court of appeal". He knew Butso had been a problem, but still tried to think of a way out, to avoid doing what he was told to do; he could not.

Dad loaded Butso in the truck and went back to the farm. He parked the truck, let Butso out, and went to get the rifle. Butso, excited by the ride, jumped up, front paws on Dad's chest, wanting to be petted.

My father knew he could not delay what had to be done. Putting it off would make it harder to do. He got the .22 from the slaughterhouse and called Butso to the hog yard. Butso, now roused, expecting to help Dad herd hogs, jumped the low hog fence, ran to Dad, tail wagging—looking into Dad's eyes—waiting for a command.

My father stood, motionless, then abruptly leveled the rifle at Butso's head and shot. But at that moment Butso moved; the bullet—instead of a kill shot to the brain—ripped through Butso's muzzle, shattering teeth and bone. Butso fell back, stunned; then, bloody and whimpering in pain, he started crawling to my father for help. Dad shot again. Butso was dead.

Years later my father told me he would never forget Butso's eyes as he crawled to him, his master, for help—or his heartache for what he had done. I can only imagine how this affected my father's feelings for Grandpa Conrad.

Dad's most beloved dog was a little black and tan Fox Terrier called "Pudgy." After he sold the meat market in 1961, Dad had time on his hands. For some reason, never explained, he got the urge to get a little housedog. He went to see Elzear O'Malley, a trucker and dog dealer, who lived on a small farm near LeCenter.

Mr. O'Malley had mostly hunting dogs, but he had a few terriers. My father was soon taken by a little year-old female that Elzear said was a good mouser.

From the time my father brought Pudgy home, until the day she died, they were seldom apart. When Dad watched TV, Pudgy was in his lap; when he went to bed, she slept on top of the bed next to him; and when he went anywhere in the car, she was with him in the front seat.

And Pudgy was good at mousing. Dad would take her to the farm. The granary was full of oats—and full of mice. Dad would lift a few floorboards and out the mice came. Pudgy would kill one mouse after the other, and eat whole one or two of them.

Pudgy was fearless. One day my father took her into a local woods while he hunted for morel mushrooms (a delicacy my parents loved fried in butter and salt and pepper). Pudgy chased a large woodchuck into a hole in the bottom of a tree. The tree leaned at an angle and was hollow to a height of about 10 feet. In her zeal, Pudgy crawled into the tree, fighting the woodchuck as it turned to face her.

My father ran to the tree. He could hear her muffled barking, snarling, and the gnashing of teeth, mixed with sharp cries of pain. The fighting was fierce.

Dad called to Pudgy to come out. Soon came a fearful realization: Pudgy could not come out. Pudgy was larger than the woodchuck and in trying to get a killing throat hold, had wedged herself into the gradually narrowing hollow tree. She could not back out.

Now Pudgy was in trouble. With her body held fast and unable to move, Pudgy was fighting at a big disadvantage. The smaller woodchuck, with room to move, was attacking Pudgy's face with sharp teeth and claws.

For Dad: What to do?

My father rushed to a nearby farmhouse and got help from the farmer. With a chain saw, they cut the dead tree down at its base, then cut it again several feet above Pudgy and the woodchuck. Then with ax and wedges, split the tree truck open, freeing dog and "chuck".

Pudgy was still game. Bleeding about the head and muzzle, she attacked the woodchuck in a frenzy—finally killing it. In a fight, she expected no quarter, and gave none.

Pudgy's devotion to my father was total. Dad never had her spayed, and she never had puppies. Even when she was "in heat," she never allowed a male dog near her.

Then in 1966, tragedy struck. It was a summer afternoon and my father was at the Slaughterhouse farm doing a few chores. He decided to drive down the dirt cattle lane to the pasture to check the herd. Pudgy was in the meadow hunting mice, so Dad did not call her to ride in the car with him. She noticed him go, however, and ran to the car, following alongside.

As Dad drove near the cattle, the car spooked a steer. Startled by the frightened animal, Pudgy jumped to the side and was caught under the wheel of the slowly moving car. My father heard a yelp, and felt a bump. He stopped and looked back—Pudgy was lying in the grass. Dad ran to Pudgy and cradled her in his arms. She gasped twice and died.

My father's grief was as if he had lost a child. He blamed himself. He should have called her to the car, and kept her in the front seat as was his habit.

Dad dug a grave next to the flower garden, wrapped Pudgy in a blanket, and gently laid her to rest. He made a wooden cross, painted it white, and added Pudgy's name. Across the top of the cross he entwined a garland of red silk roses. Pudgy was the only dog my father honored with a marked grave, and that cross remained there for years.

But it was about 10 years later, when my father was in his 70s, that a real tragedy was narrowly averted. It was during a foxhunt, and it brought Dad to the brink of killing a man over a dog.

Fox hunting, almost as dear to my father as hunting raccoon, was done in the winter with snow on the ground. In the early days, Dad's usual hunting companions were Grandpa Jim or Carl Ehmke, a Montgomery farmer and respected hunter. But now Grandpa Jim was too old and frail to hunt, and Carl Ehmke was disabled with a serious heart condition. So Dad, with only one hound (Red), was hunting alone.

When fox hunting, my father's quarry was the red fox, a beautiful animal weighing about 15 pounds with reddish fur on its back and sides, whitish fur underneath, black legs and feet, and a white-tipped tail. Common to North America, it prefers habitats that combine woods and open areas.

Red foxes spend most of their time looking for food, the main staples being mice, rabbits, ground nesting birds, and small rodents. They are largely nocturnal, becoming active about two hours before dark and ending several hours after dawn. They hunt an area of one to five square miles, frequently following cow and sheep paths (especially those leading around and through swamps), line fences, and old roads.

During the day, foxes generally sleep out in the open, dens are used only for breeding. In the winter a fox's daytime bedding area is usually located in fields, or on southern-facing slopes where it can take advantage of the sun's warmth.

It was a January afternoon, the weather mild, when my father took Red and drove to a well know red-fox territory: a hilly, wooded area adjacent to several farms and a small marshland. Dad had hunted this place many times before and knew the fox trails. With fresh snow on the ground, he could tell from fox tracks there was recent activity. He turned Red loose and went to a grove of small trees that overlooked a cow path along a line fence—and waited.

Soon Red started barking. He had jumped a fox and was hot on its trail. Most often a red fox will run for hours, but stay in the same area, circling around, using familiar trails—keeping well ahead of the dog.

Dad was on a good stand—with clear sight lines for shooting, and had killed several fox running this cow path before. He was using a 12-gauge shotgun with #4 size pellets—heavier shot than what he used for most bird shooting—but just right for fox. If Red kept the fox circling, eventually Dad hoped to get a shot.

My father listened with pleasure to Red's deep-throated baying on trail. At six years of age, Red was at the top of his hunting skills. Solid red in color and deep chested, Red was the last of Dad's hounds to carry Coke's bloodline.

As time passed, Dad could tell from Red's voice the direction the fox was going. After less than an hour, the fox had taken Red well over a mile, and now was swinging back. As Red's sound on trail got nearer, Dad stood motionless next to a tree. He was upwind from the cow path so the fox would not smell him.

Then, suddenly, my father heard the sound of a large caliber rifle blast, followed by Red's yelp of surprise and pain—then silence. Alarmed, Dad hurried out of the grove of trees and toward the sound of Red's voice and the rifle shot. Soon he came to two sets of tracks—Red and the fox—leading out of the marsh and into a bare, snow-covered cornfield. About two blocks further, he saw where Red fell, slid across the snow, and got up; then staggered, leaving a blood trail to a patch of snow churned with blood. Leading into this disturbed area were heavy boot prints and the tracks of a large dog; leading out, the bloody smear of a body being dragged to a brush pile against the line fence.

My father rushed to the brush pile and saw where scrub branches had been pulled apart, then covered with fresh snow piled on top. He tore into the pile, pulling apart the brushwood. Red's body lay crumpled, a length of intestine protruding from a bullet wound to his side. His throat was torn and matted with blood and saliva; the dog collar with Dad's name and address on the metal tag was missing.

Dad's eyes teared; rage built in waves. The story was in the snow. Someone shot Red, then commanded his dog to finish Red off. He then stripped the identifying dog collar and hid the body.

And it wouldn't be hard to find out just who that someone was. The tracks of the man and his dog were clear in the snow. Dad clutched his shotgun and followed.

The tracks led to a farm. As my father approached the farmhouse, he noticed a Shepherd dog chained to a doghouse. The shepherd dog came to the end of the chain and growled. There was blood flecked on its muzzle and shoulders, and the dog favored one leg. "Red got a piece of that bastard before he died," Dad thought.

Dad went around to the front door of the farmhouse and knocked: no answer. He knocked again: still no response. But out of the corner of his eye Dad saw a window curtain move.

"Open the damn door," my father shouted. "I've got words with you." Quiet.

Dad brought back a heavy hunting boot and banged it into the door jam. The door slammed open. A wide-eyed young man of 19 or 20 years, his face blanched with fear, stood frozen against the far kitchen wall.

My father stormed in. "You killed my dog," he shouted, bringing his shotgun to waist level and pointing it directly at the youth's belly. "I ought to gut-shoot you where you stand!"

The younger farmer was speechless, his mouth open, then stammered, "I-I'm sorry about your dog. I didn't mean to shoot him," he said, his arms outstretched in supplication. "I don't know why I did. I'm sorry. It just happened."

My father's finger curled on the trigger, held, then relaxed. He lowered the shotgun.

Some years later, as my father told the story, he would bring up his right hand with index finger and thumb spread an inch apart, "I came that close to shooting that boy," he said. "I've had nightmares ever since. I don't know how I would have lived with myself if I'd have shot him."

There was more to the story, however. In order to make amends, the young man wrote a check to my father for $125 there in the kitchen. He was farming with his parents who, at the time of the incident, were shopping in town.

Dad went home and had my mother cash the check first thing Monday morning. The young man's father, in defense of his son, went to the bank to stop payment on the check. Too late; my father had the cash.

But Dad was afraid there might be trouble. He went to Pat Smith, Sr., the long-standing and respected Sheriff of Le Sueur County, and talked it over. Sheriff Smith looked into it. The youth's father argued Dad was hunting without their permission, and that Red was shot on their cornfield. Dad argued that in 40 years of hunting, he never had to ask a farmer for permission to hunt on his property.

As it turned out, Sheriff Smith told Dad to keep the money, but next time be sure to get the farmer's okay before hunting his land. What he told the farmer and his son I don't know. My guess is that he told them the boy was lucky he didn't get shot, and that the next time they had a beef with a hunter, to call the Sheriff's office first!

10.

The String Runs Out

MY FATHER CONTINUED coon hunting until well into his 80s. By then he had sold the Slaughterhouse farm and had only one old coonhound, Spotty.

But then old age caught up to Dad as well. He lost the sight in one eye through injury (he was struck in the eye by a tree branch one night while coon hunting) and complicated by an unsuccessful cataract operation. He was having dizzy spells, had several minor car accidents, and could not drive at night. Yet he wouldn't quit. He had my mother drive him and Spotty to "Richter's Woods"—a large forested area of tall hardwood trees, downed tree limbs, and tangled underbrush about two miles from home—and drop them off. Dad would hunt the woods and then walk home.

Two events occurred, finally, to end my father's coon hunting. The first happened one night when Dad was hunting Richter's Woods. It was early in the coon-hunting season and most of the leaves were still on the trees. Spotty treed a raccoon, and Dad—in the darkness, with all the leaves, and his poor eyesight, searching with his flashlight—could not see the raccoon. To get a better look, Dad leaned his .22 rifle against a nearby log. He pushed through thick brush about 40 feet from the tree, then circled: trying to "shine" the raccoon's eyes with the light. Finally, he spotted the raccoon, but then could not remember where he laid his rifle.

Dad became disoriented. Afraid, he sat down and tried to get his bearings. Finally, his thinking cleared. A gravel road ran through the woods nearby. It would take him south to a railroad track that ran east to within a block from his house. Dad tied a big red "farmer's handkerchief to a small tree, called Spotty, and walked home. The next morning he and Mom went back and found the rifle. But the experience left my father shaken.

The final blow came several weeks later. Once again my father was going coon hunting. As he opened the car door for Spotty to jump in, the dog fell backward, unconscious. After several minutes, Spotty revived, but was unsteady on his legs as Dad led him back to the doghouse. Later Dad said Spotty had had a heart attack. Spotty was 14 years old: his hunting days were over.

One morning, not long after, my father took food and water to Spotty, but he didn't come out of his doghouse. Dad reached in—Spotty was dead—the body still warm. Dad said, "I'll not get another dog, my hunting is over."

■

FOR MY FATHER, it seems, dogs filled an emotional need seldom met in any human relationship. He might distrust the love and loyalty of another person—but not his dogs. When his last dog, Spotty, died, something went out of Dad.

Several years later, my father went into a nursing home. He became depressed, and lost interest in all the things that had given him pleasure. Then one day, the nurses said, a man brought in two puppies in a basket. A sparkle came into Dad's eyes; he smiled. He just had to touch and hold the pups.

I guess dogs do that for many people: provide that unconditional love we all yearn for and seldom find.

There were dogs in my life, but they were not as important to me as they were to my father. When I was 11 years old and my brother, Milt, six, we had a little white fox terrier with black and brown spots we called Pudgy (same name as my Dad's terrier 30 years later). He followed us everywhere.

One afternoon, as Milt and I returned home from church summer school, Pudgy was hit by a car. Seriously injured, we carried Pudgy home. My mother put him in a box with a blanket beside the wood stove. Pudgy wouldn't eat, but his stomach swelled to twice its size and turned yellow. He died five days later. In answer to our questions, Dad said, "Pudgy had something busted inside that wouldn't heal."

King was the only dog I could call my own—the Airedale and Coonhound mix. My father got him when I was 12 years old. King became mine, I think, because he had a serious shortcoming as a coonhound: he would rather fight the other dogs than hunt raccoon. He dodged a bullet from Dad only because I loved the dog; and because I was having luck hunting him on rabbits and squirrels.

When I went into the U.S. Navy, my father gave King to a farmer. The farmer said he would hunt King and use him for a watchdog. He could run free on the farm, and would not be chained to a doghouse. It was a good home. I thanked Dad for it.

King was my last dog as well. When I returned from the Navy, I got married. With college and apartment living, moves on the job, and frequent travel in retirement, Shirley and I found it inconvenient to have a dog. Perhaps when we are too old to travel, we might get a little housedog: a toy Maltese to keep us company.

Left: Dad and his dog Butso next to Uncle Bill's house on Oak Ave. W. in Montgomery, 1920s

Right: Dad with his favorite hunting dog, Coke, next to Uncle Bill's house on Oak Ave. W. in the early 1940s

My father on the right with his hunting partner, Carl Ehmke, after a successful fox hunt. Dad's using Grandpa Holey's dog, Sporty, January 1937.

Dad and his dog Red with a red fox he shot, 1973

Dad holding his dog Spotty next to Spotty's doghouse behind the garage at 504 Oak Ave. W.

IV. LEARNING *the* TRADE

Farm Hand

"**LEARNING THE TRADE**" meant learning all aspects of the Conrad Bauer and Son's business operation. When Grandpa Conrad first opened a meat market in 1889, it meant learning how to slaughter animals, prepare meat, make sausage, and serve customers. He had to buy all his meat animals from farmers.

At the turn of the century, my grandfather expanded the business by purchasing farmland around Montgomery—both as a financial investment, and as a way to grow and fatten his own meat animals for slaughter. His first purchase was 80 acres of land adjoining the city limits: the "Slaughterhouse" farm.

The farm work I did at the Slaughterhouse farm was similar to that done by the farm boys in my high school class—with one exception: I did not have to milk cows. Ours was not a dairy farm; rather its purpose was to grow feed and fatten livestock for the meat market.

Farming is cyclical in nature, and farm work is governed by the four seasons of the year beginning with spring. As soon as weather permitted, we prepared the fields for planting—a process to break up the soil, aerate and level its surface. It usually started with plowing the ground, then disking and dragging it.

Fred, our hired man, did the plowing and disking. I got stuck pretty often with dragging—that meant walking behind a team of horses pulling a flat heavy iron rake set with spikes to smooth out the ground. Once prepared, the fields were seeded in corn and oats.

For a few years, we planted a sizeable patch of potatoes. For seed we cut a potato into quarters making sure each quarter had an "eye" that would sprout into a new plant. When harvested in the fall, we filled a large bin in the basement of the meat market with potatoes and sold them off during winter.

Spring is also the season of renewal, for animals as well as crops: a time for baby chickens, pigs, and even pigeons.

In the spring my mother would get a flock of baby chicks from the hatchery in town and put them in our garage. We fed them and kept the wood stove going to keep them warm until they were old enough to take to the Slaughterhouse farm. One year Mom had 1,100 chicks.

We raised hogs. Hogs will eat almost anything. Along with corn and "slop", we fed them the blood, guts, and stomach contents of the cattle we butchered.

But raising hogs can be tricky; they are subject to many diseases. One year Dad lost the whole herd—except for one sow that survived—to hog cholera. The dead bodies were dragged into the field and burned. Mom still remembers the loss amounted to $1400.

For a few years my father tried raising pigeons. He got several pair and put them in the attic of the old chicken house. They nested and laid eggs. The young just out of the nest are called "squabs" and are tender and tasty.

My job was to fatten up the squabs by force-feeding them corn. I would put one kernel of corn in a squab's mouth and gently push it down the throat and into its crop—continuing until the crop was bulging. When fat, they were butchered. We never had enough squabs to sell in the meat market, just enough for our own table.

In late spring we had to start cultivating sweet corn. It had to be done two or three times to keep the weeds down and to help the rainfall soak into the ground. We cultivated the rows with a horse cultivator: a complicated implement with little shovels that scraped just below the surface, cutting the weeds like a hoe without hurting the roots of the corn plant.

It was a big day when my father let me climb up on the cultivator seat, grab the reins, and drive the team of horses. There was no room for error as you might end up rooting out the young seedlings instead of the weeds.

Like all our fieldwork, cultivating sweet corn was done using our one team of draft horses: Dick and Pete, two sorrel geldings weighing between 1200 and 1400 pounds each. My father did not get a farm tractor until sometime in the 1950s.

Dick, the larger of the two horses, was gentle and easygoing. Pete was feisty and harder to handle. I don't know how much love there is between two neutered male horses, but I know Pete was jealous. When work was done, the two horses were turned loose in the pasture. They were always together. If for some reason we had other horses in the pasture, Pete would fight off any suspected rival coming near Dick.

It was easy to get attached to horses. Our hired man, Fred, threatened to quit if my father ever sold Dick and Pete, saying, "If they go; I go!" Eventually Dad did get rid of the horses and bought a Ford tractor. Fred didn't quit.

During the summer months we cut and stacked hay, harvested sweet corn, and threshed oats.

We had two hay fields on the Slaughterhouse farm: one field seeded in alfalfa, the other in timothy. It was the principal winter food for our cattle and horses.

Fred used a riding hay mower pulled by Dick and Pete to cut the hay. The sharp blades of the mower cut close to the ground and could be dangerous. More than one ring-necked pheasant hen had its head cut off as it hunkered down over a nest of eggs and would not fly off. In the thick grasses, Fred could not see the pheasant until it was too late.

And my mother told of a terrible thing that happened involving a hay mower on a small farm near Montgomery. A young farmer was mowing hay when his toddler son stumbled out into the deep grass in front of the mower. Before the farmer could stop the horses, the mower cut off the little boy's feet. The town doctor was called, and upon arriving found the farmer sitting on the front steps of the farmhouse—moaning and rocking back and forth—holding the dead child in his arms. With tears in his eyes, he beseeched the doctor to "sew the feet back on."

During the summer, we could get two or three cuttings of hay. Once cut, the hay was left on the field several days to dry or cure in the sun—then raked into windrows.

We stored the hay in two pole barns—one at the Slaughterhouse feedlot, and the other near the hay field—and in hay stacks. When the hay was dry—it had to be dry when stored or it became moldy and unfit for cattle feed—it was raked into piles, loaded onto a hay wagon, and hauled to the pole barns. Usually I rode the hay wagon; driving the horses from pile to pile as Fred, with hay fork in had, pitched hay in the wagon and I "made the load."

Often we had an extra hired man to help with haying. When we stored hay in haystacks on the field, my job was to "buck" the hay to the side of the stack with a horse-drawn hay rake. Then one man pitched the hay to another man on the haystack. He built it up and finally topped it off.

However, what I remember most about haying was the heat, the sweat, and Mom's ice-cold lemonade and sandwiches. As the saying goes, "You make hay when the sun shines," which usually meant hot and humid as well.

But I was fortunate. The heat didn't seem to bother me as much as it did the others; I did not sweat. I can still see our hired men, their shirts soaked through, and rivulets of perspiration running down their cheeks and dripping off their noses as they worked. And my shirt was dry. Men sweat; and I felt I had arrived one day when the underarms of my shirt were wet too.

About midday a most welcome sight was our 1941 Chevrolet slowly coming down the cattle lane and through the woods to the hay field. It was my mother with a basket of sandwiches and a big thermos of lemonade. Mom's sandwich recipe was Tastee white bread spread thick with mayonnaise and slices of minced ham in between. We would all sit under the shade of oak trees near the pole barn and enjoy. It was a much-needed break and chance to get out of the noonday sun.

During the month of August, sweet corn was ripe and ready to be picked. For years, Conrad Bauer and Sons had a contract with the Minnesota Valley Canning Company to sell them our sweet corn. When our field was ready, MVCC would come with horse-drawn wagons and crews of Mexican workers. As the wagons were pulled slowly through the cornfield, workers on either side of the wagon would hand pick the corn and fling the ears into the wagon. With corn stalks well over six feet tall, often the only way to tell where a wagon was in the field was to look for the high flying ears.

Summer was also time to thresh oats on our 40-acre farm north of town. My father contracted with Adolph Trcka of Montgomery to do the threshing. Adolph brought his threshing machine, power-driven by a tractor. Once the machine was set up, we went into the field and loaded the bundles in a hayrack. The load of bundles was brought next to the machine, and one man pitched one bundle at a time into the threshing machine feeder.

Sometimes I hauled bundles in from the field, but mostly my job was pitching bundles in to the threshing machine. The bundles were not heavy, but there was some skill required to this chore. Ideally, the bundles lined up on the feeder, head to tail, with the heads going in first. It was important not to pile the bundles into the feeder; it would choke, then you had to shut everything down and clean out the machine.

The threshing machine separated the oat kernels from the straw—blowing the oats into a truck box and the straw into a huge straw pile. The oats were taken to the Slaughterhouse farm and put into a granary for use as horse, chicken, or hog feed. The straw was used for bedding in the cattle barn.

During the winter months, farming for Conrad Bauer and Sons involved feeding the livestock at the Slaughterhouse farm feed lot and hauling out the manure.

Along with hay and corn, a very important food for our cattle was silage (ensilage) that we got from the Minnesota Valley Canning Company. In processing sweet corn, MVCC would strip the corn kernels from the corn ears. The remaining leaves and corncobs were piled on a huge mound and allowed to ferment. This juicy mixture—succulent and vitamin-rich—developed a deep golden aroma, rich and sour, like tobacco cured with rum. We hauled it to the feedlot by the truckload. The cattle loved it.

The obvious problem that develops when you feed haystacks of hay, truckloads of silage, bushel baskets of corn, and sacks of oats to over 100 head of cattle along with hogs, horses, and chickens is manure—and lots of it. During the winter months, we put down straw for bedding in the cattle barn and horse stable. This straw mixed with animal excrement was the manure that had to be hauled out on a regular basis.

Cleaning the barn was a dirty job and was done by hand. Using a five-tine fork, we shoveled the manure into an automatic manure spreader, hauled it out onto the cornfield, and spread it as fertilizer.

In winter the outdoor feedlot created a problem. The ground around the feeding troughs built up with layer upon layer of frozen feces and urine mixed with snow and ice. This manure could not be dug up and hauled out until spring thaw—and then the melt created a foot deep soupy quagmire. Too watery to haul and spread, we had to wait until such time as the manure was sufficiently dry. All and all, the most unpleasant job in farming.

The Cattle Drive

IN THE AUTUMN, it was time for the five-mile cattle drive from the pasture at the St. Michael farm to the winter feedlot at the Slaughterhouse farm. For a kid like me it was cowboy time. But first, a brief history and description of the farm.

In the *Montgomery Messenger*, dated January 21, 1999, in its "Messenger Memories" feature (80 years ago—January 17, 1919) appeared this historical note: "Conrad Bauer purchased seventy acres of land from Frank Kral, near St. Michael's church, for which he paid $110.00 per acre."

That 70 acres, as I knew it in the 1930s and early 40s, was mostly pasture, enclosed by barbwire fence. It had several acres of marshland on the south end and a dozen or so acres of woodland on the west. St. Michael's church was gone, but the small cemetery (just north of the woods and adjacent to the pasture) was still maintained and used by a number of Irish Catholic families living in the area. A narrow gravel road ran north and south along the west side of the farm, from which a rutted dirt road entered; running through the woods and down into a sheltered hollow within which stood a two-room log house, a small log cattle barn, and a corral. A deep well, with power from a gas engine, pumped water into a stock tank for the cattle. Joe "Dutch," a middle aged immigrant from Austria, lived in the log house and did work for Grandpa Conrad.

In the spring, up to 100 head of young feeder steers were purchased at the South St. Paul Stockyards and trucked out to the St.
Michael farm. The steers would spend the summer and early fall
filling out on grass, then be driven to the Slaughterhouse feedlot
to fatten on corn, silage, and hay during the winter, and finally
killed off as needed for the meat market.

The problem Grandpa Conrad faced early on was how to
transport the cattle from St. Michael's to the Slaughterhouse farm.
These steers were wild, having been raised on the Western plains
and shipped by rail to South St. Paul. And for six months they ran
free on pasture without much human contact. Getting them into
trucks was nearly impossible.

So the decision was made to form a cattle drive: to drive the
herd of steers down county gravel roads from the one farm to
the other. In the 1920s, my father and Paul Ehmke, a hired man,
rode on horseback as cowboys driving the herd. In later years I
remember the excitement when Dad threw his Texas saddle on
Dolly, our dapple-gray mare, pulled the cinch tight, and swung
aboard—starting off the drive.

An obvious problem on a drive was how to keep spirited and
untamed steers on the road and moving ahead, instead of running
off into some farmer's field, or worse, if spooked, stampeding
through fences and damaging farm property along the way—certainly not good business for Conrad Bauer and Sons. There was
a solution, however, based on the tendency of cattle to follow a
leader. And that brings us to the story of one aristocrat I'll call
"Old Red."

In one of the first herds brought to the St. Michael farm, Joe
Dutch noticed a natural leader emerge: a rangy, mixed-breed
Shorthorn steer the others followed from pasture to water tank
and back. Red in color with white markings, he had a commanding
presence the others were drawn to. Docile, he sought human

contact—coming up to Joe on the front steps of the log house and eating ears of corn from Joe's hand—whereas the other steers were wary and skittish. During the long summer, Red became Joe's pet. He followed Joe around and liked Joe to rub his neck and scratch his head. Joe wondered about this. Perhaps Red, as a calf on the Western plains, lost his mother and was bottle-fed by some rancher's daughter, or some such account.

When the fall cattle drive started, Red took the lead and walked down the road with the rest of the herd in tow. With a horseman ahead of the herd and several walking behind, the five-mile drive was completed without incident. That fall, and for some years after, Red played the Judas Goat, leading the herd to the feedlot and death, saving his life at the expense of others.

But time came for change. Old Red had grown solitary and was slow to lead the herd to water. A young steer was vying for herd leadership. So it was decided the coming fall cattle drive would be Red's last.

That winter, the day came for Old Red to face the same fate as those he had led. But who would pull the trigger on Red and slit his throat? He was not only Joe's pet, he was like family. Although my father did not like the job, he knew he had to do it. When the time came, it was said, Old Red followed Dad into the slaughterhouse with his head held high—facing death without a tremor of fear—like the leader he was. My guess was Old Red followed Dad thinking he might get an ear of corn and his head scratched.

Following World War II, the end of Bauer's cattle drives was in sight. Farmers and homeowners living along the route of the drive no longer tolerated the trail of excrement left by the herd. In 1947, George Brunner, Grandpa Conrad's old friend, put the changed attitude into words: "The cowboy days are over; these cattle drives have got to stop," as he watched helplessly as the hooves of a dozen steers trampled his lawn and garden. And they were stopped. After that, modern trucks were used to haul the steers; and those too wild to be loaded were shot in the pasture and dragged into the truck.

Other childhood memories crowd my mind about the St. Michael farm: going with Dad each week to count the herd to make sure no steer had gotten through the fence and run off; getting a kick out of my father as he bawled like a mother cow calling her calf and brought the whole herd on a run to him; swearing at the gasoline motor that pumped water into the stock tank as once again it wouldn't start; with Fred, digging fence-post holes and fixing the fence that surrounded the farm; and eating chunks of potato and eggs fried in bacon grease with Joe Dutch—and Joe.

13.

Joe Dutch

YOU COULD WRITE a whole book about Joe Dutch. As a young immigrant from Austria, he came to the United States just before World War I to escape military service. He promised his sweetheart he would come back after the war and they would marry. When he returned to Austria, to his dismay he found his girlfriend already married—to his brother. Angry, he almost committed suicide by jumping off a bridge. But instead, he returned to the U.S. and the Montgomery area.

With difficulty speaking English, little schooling, and no skills, getting a job was Joe's first priority. He was willing to work, however, and soon got odd jobs: helping farmers with haying and threshing grain, digging trenches for tile to drain wet lands, and digging graves and cutting lawns at St. Michael's Cemetery. With a long Germanic name that was hard to pronounce, the Irish and Czech famers called him Joe "Dutch."

But Joe wanted a steady job and a place to stay. And he had luck. One of the first stops he made on arriving in Montgomery was Bauer's Meat Market. Grandpa Conrad had just purchased the St. Michael farm and needed someone to live in the log house, keep an eye on the steers, and make sure the stock tank was full of water. Joe got the job.

When I knew Joe Dutch, he was in his early 60s and walked with a stoop. He had close cropped black hair sprinkled with gray, a creased face tanned by sun to the color of beef jerky, and the rough hands of a man used to working with a hay fork and digging spade.

A gentle man, I never knew Joe to smoke, drink, or shoot a gun. He was shy, yet friendly with a smile that brightened his whole face. I liked him.

Joe lived in one room of the two-room log house with a bed, table, two chairs, and a cast iron woodstove. The other room housed his laying hens. His only light came from a kerosene lamp on the table.

I think Joe lived on liver sausage, eggs, and potatoes—all fried in a deep, iron fry pan with half an inch of bacon grease; the congealed grease remained in the pan until heated for the next meal. He used a slice or two of bread to wipe his plate clean.

Joe had a large blue enamel coffee pot, blackened from years of use, half filled with old coffee grounds. When he made coffee, Joe just added a pinch of fresh coffee grounds and water to whatever coffee was left in the pot—and heated. He didn't believe in waste.

Yet I loved Joe's food, particularly the potatoes. In those days, most people just boiled potatoes and mashed them. Joe, instead, cut the potatoes in chunks and dropped the pieces into hot grease— somewhat like French fried potatoes are made today—then when done, added plenty of salt and pepper. The words cholesterol and saturated fat were then known only to scientists.

Every few weeks, Joe would walk the five miles to town for groceries; he never owned a car and did not know how to drive. Neighboring farmers seeing him walking along the road would offer him a ride, but he never accepted. No one knew why he refused; he wasn't walking for his health. My guess is that Joe did not want to be beholden to anyone.

Although well liked, Joe was a private person, content to live alone. He never talked about himself or discussed his innermost feelings. He had an ironic sense of humor, however, that came out in a grisly story he told about the death of a neighbor.

Bill C., a man much like Joe, lived alone in a one-room shack on the edge of a marsh about a half mile from Joe. They were not close friends, but loneliness or simply the need for occasional human contact would bring one on a visit to the other.

It was a hot and sticky July afternoon when Joe waked over to visit Bill. He hadn't seen Bill for several weeks and had some concern. Joe knocked on the door: no answer. He knocked several more times; then, thinking Bill asleep shouted, "Bill, are you dead in there?" Still no answer. Troubled, Joe tried the door, and then pushed it open. An overpowering stench blew him back. Bill's bloated body, the buttons popping off his shirt, lay barely recognizable in bed. He had been dead for days.

When telling the tale, Joe would repeat how he shouted out, "Bill, are you dead in there?" Then with a wry smile and chuckle add, "And by God—he was."

When my father sold the meat market in 1961, he put the St. Michael farm up for sale. Joe was in his 70s now: too old for farm labor and in need of a home. By this time Joe had become part of our "family," so Dad found a little one-room shanty for Joe and moved it onto the Slaughterhouse farm. Mom made sure he had groceries, and Joe kept an eye on the livestock and took care that the dogs and chickens had water. Joe was happy.

Several years went by. Joe was in his 80s and doing fine. Then one day my mother heard the hounds howling and barking in a frenzy. She went to investigate and found Joe on the ground near the dog kennel—unable to get up.

My father took Joe to the hospital. The doctor said he had had a stroke and had "hardening of the arteries" (arteriosclerosis)— saying the arteries in Joe's forearms were like small glass pipes.

Joe recovered enough to be transferred to a small nursing home in Montgomery. But within a few months, a series of small strokes brought on dementia, and an extreme personality change. Joe became paranoid, thinking staff members and other patients were trying to steal his money, and aggressive, grabbing at nurses as they walked by. He was adjudged mentally ill and committed to the St. Peter State Hospital.

Although Joe had a picture of Jesus Christ and a palm frond on the wall of his house, he never professed a religious belief. As Joe lay dying during the last days of his life, a Roman Catholic priest came to give him the "Last Rites." Joe would have none of that, however, telling the priest, "Don't push it. I'm not ready to go yet."

My parents were not aware of Joe's death until weeks after. Without relatives or assets, Joe was buried in a potter's field on the hospital grounds. When word got back to Montgomery, several farm families in the area wanted Joe disinterred and buried in St. Michael Cemetery. But the cost of $500 to do that put an end to further discussion.

I have one tangible reminder of Joe Dutch: his kerosene lamp. When Joe died, my parents kept the lamp, and years later gave it to me. The lamp was just as Joe left it: the glass chimney soot stained and the flat wick patched with black sewing thread. My wife Shirley cleaned it up and on occasion brings it in from the garage, a relic of a bygone time.

14.

Blood and Guts

BEFORE I GO INTO the technical details of butchering livestock for market (some of which may be repugnant to readers), I should discuss the emotions aroused by this work and the attitudes about it.

Just the words "slaughter" and "butcher" have unpleasant connotations. *Webster's New Collegiate Dictionary* has several meanings for slaughter including this: "to kill in a bloody or violent manner." The word butcher includes the meaning: "one that kills ruthlessly or brutally."

Although most people in this country like to eat meat, they don't like to think about the process that puts the hamburger in their Big Mac, or the ham on the Sunday dinner table. They know the meat comes from an animal, but they do not want to know how the animal was killed. Sure the friendly meat cutter dressed in starch white in the meat department of their neighborhood supermarket is decent enough, but what kind of man works in a slaughterhouse killing animals? Surely these men must be uneducated and callous—brutal even, and maybe perverse, enjoying the killing.

I cannot speak for butchers in general, but for my father, our hired men, and myself, slaughtering livestock was work— not pleasant and not fun. Killing was to be quick and efficient. Tormenting an animal for no reason before killing was abhorrent.

When we killed and dressed cattle, it was done on the Slaughterhouse farm. The slaughterhouse itself was a rough, unpainted one-room wood-frame building with three doors: a front door large enough to load quarters of beef onto a truck, a side door that opened into a corral, and a small sliding door in the back that opened into the hog yard—and no windows.

The room inside the slaughterhouse was about the size of an average living room with a high ceiling. With the doors closed, the only light came from a single, dust-covered light bulb hanging from the ceiling. A large wooden windlass anchored on a four-foot high platform was along one side of the room, and a row of pegs for coveralls and a wooden holder for skinning knives and a sharpening steel on the other side. The elevated wooden floor, encrusted with an accumulation of dried blood and animal waste, had a V-shaped trough running down its center and out the back door.

Butchering an animal (steer, bull, or cow) was best done by two men. The animal was first separated from the herd, then driven from the cattle barn and into the corral. One man with a .22 rifle went into the slaughterhouse and got up on the four-foot high platform. The other man herded the animal up a ramp and into the slaughterhouse through the side door. It was then shot, skinned out, quartered, and hauled to the meat market in town.

In the summer we butchered during the cool of the evening: shirtless with only work pants and suspenders. In winter, since the slaughterhouse was not heated, we wore heavy coveralls. We worked with bare hands kept warm from handling steaming entrails and body parts.

I started helping my father in the slaughterhouse when I was about six years old: doing little chores like sweeping the blood off the floor, bringing water to wash off the beef carcass, and holding the tail and head as Dad skinned each out. As I got older, I helped skin out the carcass and quarter it.

One day, when I was about 12 years old, my father said it was time for me to be the shooter. It was during the war and we were butchering cattle at a record pace: up to 14 head a week to supply Minnesota Valley Canning Company with meat. My father had a Black Angus steer in the corral to be killed.

I went into the slaughterhouse, climbed up on the windlass platform, and jacked a cartridge into the single shot .22 rifle we kept in the corner. Dad was in the corral with a pitchfork to goad the steer in.

In most cases, getting an animal into the slaughterhouse was no problem. Just the touch of a sharp pitchfork tine to the rump handled a steer's reluctance. But there were times... I remember one such case: an angry bull with horns and weighing about 1500 pounds. My father could not get the bull into the corral without the bull charging at him. We couldn't shoot the bull in the corral and drag him into the slaughterhouse—he was too big. Finally Dad shot the bull in each foot, in the soft part just above the hoof. The bull could still walk, but the pain was such that the fight was out of him and he went into the slaughterhouse with no trouble.

My father had no problem herding the Angus steer into the darkened killing room. He closed the door and waited.

Inside, I was quiet and stood still. As was common, the steer was confused by the dim light and unsettled by the strong odor of dried blood. He smelled along the side of the wall and on the floor. I waited until he settled down. Then, in a normal voice I called out, "Ha ha" to get his attention. The steer turned and looked up to the sound of my voice. I raised the rifle to my shoulder and, as Dad had taught me, aimed at a point just above the center of the steer's forehead (a point where the lines from the base of the horns to the eyes should cross) and shot.

Upon impact of the .22 rifle slug, the steer dropped to the floor as if hit with a sledgehammer, and rolled to one side. The steer's eyes rolled back in its head, and his whole body trembled.

At the sound of the rifle shot and the steer's body hitting the floor, Dad opened the side door, rushed in and grabbed a skinning knife. As the steer shuddered, Dad pulled its head back and slashed its throat from ear to ear—and deep to the spinal column, cutting through carotid arteries and jugular vein. Blood gushed out and squirted two feet in the air. As Dad stepped back, the steer's body convulsed, the legs kicking violently in throes of death.

At this point you might ask: "Wasn't there a better way to kill cattle?" and "Wasn't it dangerous to be in a room with such an animal, the doors closed, and the only thing between you and the steer or bull was a four-foot platform and a .22 single shot rifle?" I say no to the first question, and yes to the second.

Actually, shooting was not the usual way of killing cattle in those days. The big meat packing companies first stunned the animal with a hammer before cutting its throat. Upton Sinclair in his powerful novel *The Jungle* (1906) described this method in his exposé of Chicago's meat packing industry: An animal was put in a narrow pen with no room to turn around. A man, called a "knocker" and armed with a sledgehammer, stood above the pen and struck the animal in the head before a butcher bled it.

When my grandfather first started butchering, he used the flat end of an ax or a sledgehammer to stun cattle. I remember the slaughterhouse still had an iron bullring bolted to the floor to aid in this purpose. Grandpa Conrad would throw a rope around the animal's head, string the end through the ring, and pull the animal's head down to position it for the blow.

By the time my father was butchering, a rifle was used to kill the animal. Trying to lasso an angry bull, weighing as much as 2,000 pounds, then getting him under control enough to knock him unconscious with an ax was time consuming—and dangerous.

And yes it could be dangerous to be in the slaughterhouse with an animal. Sometimes a bull, angry and confused, would go after the shooter on the platform. If that happened, we had a handrail and ledge above the platform to grab and lift ourselves out of harm's way. But I can't recall anyone being hurt. My father was careful with animals—he did not trust them—and he taught the hired men and me well.

There were close calls though. One such incident happened when I was away in the Navy. An elderly farmer from near LeCenter had been killed by a bull. The man, living with his married son on the family farm, had raised the bull from a calf, pampering it like a pet. The huge Holstein bull, always docile, was kept in a pen in the barn. Each morning the famer, as was his habit, went into the pen with the bull to feed and curry him—a pleasing ritual for the farmer, and seemingly for the bull as well.

Then one morning for some reason the bull turned violent and, in a rage, rammed the farmer against the barn wall. Hearing the commotion, the son rushed into the barn to see his father down, the bull goring him with its horns. The son was too late; his father was dead.

The next day the son called my father. He wanted the bull out of his sight and off the property. Dad purchased the bull with plans to butcher him in a week's time.

To my brother Milt, this was high drama: Dad was going to butcher a man-killer. He shared the news with a couple of junior high school friends, and they made plans to witness the bull's comeuppance.

On the day of the "execution," Milt and his friends stood behind the corral fence in high expectation. Dad was in the slaughterhouse, rifle in hand, as Fred prepared to drive the black and white bull inside. The boys were tense with anxiety: Would the bull go after Fred?

Surprisingly, the bull was submissive and went up the ramp into the slaughterhouse without resistance. Somewhat disappointed, the boys waited for a rifle shot and the sound of a body hitting the floor.

Then suddenly, they heard a bellow of rage and saw a splintering of boards as the wild-eyed bull crashed through the front door and charged out into the yard like a fighting bull in Spain entering the bullring. Scared witless, the boys broke for the front cattle gate and escaped to safety.

As Milt and his friends watched, my father calmly stepped out the shattered slaughterhouse door and faced the crazed beast. As the bull prepared to charge, Dad, like a white hunter in one of Ernest Hemmingway's stories about big game hunting in Africa, coolly sighted in and dropped the killer with a single shot.

To this day, we don't know what set off the bull, what maddened him. But it was an example of the unpredictability of livestock—especially of bulls—and my father's wisdom in being cautious while handling them.

So after my father cut the black Angus steer's throat and the body had stopped convulsing, we skinned out and removed the head, then rolled the carcass onto its back. The legs were skinned out and severed at the knee, and then the skin of the carcass was split over the midline from the breast to the rectum. Now with Dad on one side of the carcass and me on the other, we began skinning down the sides.

My father was like a surgeon with a skinning knife. With his left hand pulling the hide tightly toward him and the right hand taking steady down-strokes with the knife, he would have the whole side of the carcass stripped in a matter of minutes.

As with all Dad's knives—whether the curved broad-bladed skinning knife, the straight and narrow-bladed boning knife, or the long-bladed butcher knife—they had to be sharp; literally like a razor. Dad taught me how to sharpen a knife, using a three-sided oilstone and sharpening steel, and how to keep them sharp. To check my work, he would take one of my knives and try to shave the hair from his forearm—if he couldn't, the knife was too dull. With his instruction, I got to be pretty good with a knife.

After the steer's sides had been skinned down, we opened the carcass at the belly and pulled the small intestines out to one side. We used a saw to open the brisket and pelvis. Then with iron hooks through hind hocks, we used the windlass to raise the hindquarters off the floor. Intestines and paunch were cut free and dragged out the small rear door, down a ramp and into the hog yard.

By this time in the butchering process, the hogs were in a frenzy. When the steer's throat was cut, the hot blood ran down the trough and out into the hog yard. The hogs went wild, fighting each other to drink the blood. Now as I pulled the viscera into the hog yard with a four-pronged long handled hook, a dozen or more hogs, squealing and maddened with hunger, swarmed around me tearing chunks of flesh from the huge belly and pulling strings of entrails in frantic tugs of war. It didn't take long for the hogs to devour the steer's paunch and intestines as well as the partially digested food within.

A hog's craving for blood and flesh led to some gruesome incidents. One story I recall had a middle-aged farmer going into the barn to feed corn to his hogs. When he did not return for supper, his wife went to the barn and, to her horror, saw her husband's body jerking beneath a cluster of hogs in a feeding frenzy. His face and most of his internal organs had been eaten away. A medical report suggested the farmer might have had a stroke or heart attack with bleeding from a fall. Smelling blood, the hogs assaulted and began feeding on the paralyzed or unconscious man.

With half the steer's carcass raised off the floor, Dad and I skinned the back of the thighs. Dad removed the steer's penis by cutting it off at the anus.

With bulls, the genitals are truly remarkable. A bull's flaccid penis is long—the length of a man's arm from shoulder to finger tips—and snaky, like an oversized garden hose. As a boy, I sometimes used it like a bullwhip to ward off hogs as I dragged guts into the hog yard. The pendulous testicles are large, each about six inches long and in the shape of a small football, big enough to fill a man's hand. When cut in half, the flesh of the testicle is the color and texture of the meat of a ripe peach. We heard bulls' testicles, called "Rocky Mountain oysters," were said by some to be good eating. Although we never tasted them, the hogs ate them with relish.

Other organs were removed from the steer: liver, heart, lungs, and esophagus. The liver, whether from cattle, hogs, or calves, was kept and sold over the counter in the meat market. Liver, especially calves' liver, was considered very nutritious and frequently pre-scribed by physicians to their patients in treating iron-deficiency anemia. Hearts were either sold over the counter or used in making hamburger. My mother would cut up a heart and use it, like squirrel or rabbit meat, in making Vomacka, the Czech sour cream soup. The lungs and esophagus had no use in the meat market and were fed to my father's hounds or to the hogs.

Now the steer's tail was skinned out, the back skinned down, and the carcass hoisted off the floor. Then Dad took a two-handed meat saw and split the steer in half through the center of the backbone.

While my father was sawing the steer in half, I took the wheel barrel and hauled the steer's 60-pound hide to the "hide house"—a small room with a cement floor that was attached to the cattle barn. I stretched the hide, hair side down, over a stack of hides from cattle butchered over the previous few weeks. With a small scoop shovel, I covered the hide with a thin layer of crushed rock salt to cure it.

Stretching and salting down bloody cattle hides during most of the year was just another dirty job that had to be done, but during the hot summer months it got real unpleasant. The hide house had no windows and no ventilation so the heat buildup inside was intense. The suffocating stench of hot fetid air that hit you upon opening the door was enough to stagger a man.

And then there were the flies: the big bluebottle blowflies with bulbous iridescent blue-green abdomens that swarmed on the pile of hides. The female flies laid eggs that covered the exposed flesh like grains of salt from a saltshaker and within 24 hours became maggots—the squirmy little white worms that fed on bits of meat and blood clinging to the hides. All in all, not a pretty scene.

Our hides were sold to the Mengelkoch Company, a rendering firm from the Twin Cities, that sent out a truck about once a month to pick up the hides as well as bones, tallow, and grease. Before the truck was loaded, we would "shake out" each hide. One man would take the front of the hide and the other the back and then beat it against the hide house wall—shaking out rock salt and maggots. The salt was reused; and the door to the hide house left open for the chickens to come in and clean up the maggots.

By the time I was done salting the hide, my father had finished splitting the steer in half. He backed the Model A Ford pickup truck to the front door of the slaughterhouse and laid a heavy canvas tarp over the truck box. Now it was time to load the carcass: time for heavy lifting.

To get an idea of the weight of the carcass: The live weight or weight "on the hoof" of cattle we butchered ranged from about 1,000 to as high as 2,000 pounds. After the animal was butchered, the "dressed" weight, or weight after the animal had been skinned and eviscerated, was about 60 percent of the live weight. Our Angus steer weighed about 1,200 pounds as he walked into the slaughterhouse. The dressed weight of his carcass was 720 pounds and each half 360 pounds.

To load the carcass into the pickup, my father had to separate the two halves into quarters. As the two sides of the beef were hanging, suspended off the floor by hooks through the hocks, Dad cut each between the ribs, leaving about six inches of flank meat attached to keep the two front or forequarters from falling to the floor. Then as Dad got a hold of one front quarter, I severed the remaining flank meat and 180 pounds of fresh meat dropped into his arms. I watched as my father staggered the several steps to the truck and heaved the quarter of beef into the canvas-covered box. In like manner the other front quarter was loaded. Then as Dad in turn wrapped his arms around each hindquarter and raised it enough for me to pull the windlass hooks out, they too were loaded.

Watching my father lift and heave quarters of beef, the muscles along his arms and neck swelling, proved to me his strength. Dad's 145 pounds formed a compact bundle of muscle and sinew with nary an ounce of fat to be seen. And Dad was quick and agile too. If he were in high school today, I could visualize him as a star wrestler or outstanding goalie in ice hockey.

As strong as he was, my father never looked for a fight. His natural reaction was to walk away from an argument before it escalated into a physical confrontation. There was an exception though, and my brother Milt was there when that exception took place.

It happened in the Palace Bar next to the meat market. Milt was about six years old and Dad in his early 40s. They were walking through the bar when confronted by a farmer, "Herman." Except for the bartender and a few other patrons, the saloon was empty. Herman, a tall and rangy man in his 30s, was leaning on the long oak bar with one foot on the brass railing. He was drunk. As my father approached, Herman lurched away from the bar and stepped in front of Dad saying he had a score to settle. Dad ignored the farmer and attempted to walk around him. Herman grabbed Dad's arm and started calling him names. Words were exchanged. As my father jerked his arm away, the drunken farmer slapped Dad's face, a challenge no man could ignore.

Milt remembers the next few moments as a blur: Dad throwing punches—felt hats flying—Herman going down and out, his head resting against a brass spittoon, blood trickling from his nose and one ear. And Dad standing, his fists doubled, waiting for Herman to get up. But the fight was over; the farmer needed help getting to his feet.

Milt laughed as he recalled being so nervous he picked up both felt hats and, by mistake, gave Herman's hat to Dad and Dad's to Herman.

To this day neither Mom nor Milt can remember the nature of Herman's grievance with Dad. As to the outcome of the fight, I recalled talk that Herman's father was going to sue Dad, but nothing came of it.

After my father and I finished loading the steer's carcass into the pickup, we drove to town and through the alley to the back of the meat market. I opened the large wooded floor-to-ceiling vertical folding doors of the back room and Dad backed the truck in.

The back room, where we scalded hogs and butchered poultry and calves, had a cement floor and drain, and an overhead iron railing. The railing ran through the back room, down a long narrow hallway adjacent to the sausage room, and into the cutting room and walk-in cooler. Each beef quarter was hoisted onto a hook (attached to a wheel) and rolled down the railing and into the cooler where the meat was chilled and aged.

Aging beef quarters meant keeping them undisturbed at a temperature a few degrees above freezing for a week or so to allow the meat to ripen—to become more tender and flavorful—before cutting them up into steaks, roasts, and ribs.

The steer's head was taken into the sausage room and laid on the long wooden worktable. My father first cut out the tongue, then took an iron cleaver and split the head in half. He gently scooped out the soft, gray, pulpy brain, peeled off the covering membrane, and put it into the white porcelain sink with the tail, tongue, heart, and liver to soak in cold water. Then Dad took a boning knife and carved off the heavy cheek meat from each side of the head and tossed them into a galvanized metal tub to be added with other beef trimmings and ground into hamburger.

Beef brains, the meaty part of tails, and tongues were sold over the counter. My mother's recipe for beef brains was to dice them, scramble with eggs, and fry in butter. Fred loved a plate full for breakfast—a pleasure I did not share. Beef tails were severed at the joints and sold for making oxtail soup: a frequent meal at our house and one I did enjoy.

One day when I was 14 years old, about two years after butchering the black Angus steer, I asked my father to let me butcher a "beef" from start to finish—alone. It was a day, not out of the ordinary, and we had an animal to slaughter—a steer, bull, or cow—and Dad was about to run the animal into the slaughterhouse with me to do the shooting. As he turned to go into the corral, on impulse I took his arm and said, "Pa, let me butcher this one by myself. Just help me roll it on its back after I bleed it, then go do chores. I'll call you when its time to load the quarters."

Dad smiled at me, nodded and said, "Sure Bart, have a go at it."

I finished with no problem and when it was time to load the quarters into the truck, I called Dad. He took a good look at the meat and said, "You did good." That night he told my mother.

"He was proud of you," Mom told me later. To her dying day, Mom remembered that occasion clearly.

After cattle, swine (hogs and pigs) were the most important meat animals we slaughtered. Swine are generally classified by age. The young are called pigs and the more mature are called hogs. The flesh of these carcasses is called pork. For ease of discussion I will use the term hogs.

Most of the hogs we slaughtered were less than a year old and weighed between 175 and 250 pounds. They were shot and bled in the cattle barn, loaded into the pickup, and hauled to the back room of the meat market, then scalded and dressed.

The procedure for butchering a hog had to be done with skill to avoid carcass waste. The man doing the sticking used a boning knife with a straight and narrow blade, about eight inches long, with a sharp point. Instead of cutting the hog's throat from ear to ear, the sticker thrust the blade into the hog's throat just in front of the breast bone and down at a 40-degree angle—driving the blade to the hilt under the breast bone; then a thrust upward toward the head to sever the carotid artery. If done right, the blood spurted out; if not, the procedure had to be repeated.

My father had strong words about "shoulder sticking" a hog—a rookie blunder. It was important that the knife go straight into the hog's throat (in line with its backbone) and not off to one side or the other and into a shoulder, thereby causing the blood to settle in the shoulder and making the bloody meat unusable.

Once the hog was bled, each man took a leg and pulled the carcass into the flat bottom of the truck. The hog was taken to the back room of the meat market and dragged onto a heavy wooden bench. A large wooden barrel was rolled next to the bench and filled with hot water from the gas-heated kettle in our sausage room. A block-and-tackle was used to raise and lower the carcass into the barrel of steaming water (about 165 degrees) until the hair was loosened and could be pulled out by hand. The hog was then laid on the bench. Each man took a special hog scraper, called a bell scraper, and scraped the hair off the carcass. Bristles that couldn't be scraped off were shaved off with a knife.

Fred was particularly proud of his work on a hog. When he finished scraping and shaving, he'd run his hands caressingly over the smooth white body and say, "Slick as a baby's ass."

Once the hog was scraped clean, the carcass was hoisted up and hung from the back legs on hooks on the overhead railing. The hog was gutted, sawed in half, and rolled into the walk-in cooler.

It is said that when butchering hogs, you can use everything but the squeal. My father did not go that far, but in some way just about every part of the hog carcass had value. After the carcass had been chilled in the cooler for a day or two, Lindy Linberger or Dad cut the hog into pork ribs, roasts, chops, and steaks. The boneless section of fat and meat behind the ribs was cut away for bacon. The excess fat was trimmed off, ground, cooked, and rendered into lard. The hog's jowls, ears, and tail were cooked and went into liver sausage, blood sausage, or headcheese. The hog's stomach was washed and scraped clean—inside and out—and used as an edible container for headcheese. Like beef, the tongue, heart, and liver were utilized.

When butchering cattle I worked mostly with my father, but when it came to hogs—it was either Fred or one other hired man I'll call Tom. Tom, in his 20s, was not married and liked girls. Scraping and gutting hogs in a steaming back room opened the door for much ribald humor. If it wasn't an off-colored joke involving a hog's body part, it was his philosophy about women. He bragged that he was going with two girls and having sexual relations with each. I was about 15 years old then and did not think that was right. Finally I said to Tom, "You should marry one or the other, not lead them both on like this."

Tom laughed and said, "That I will, and it'll be the first one that gets knocked up!"

I had trouble understanding that line of reasoning.

We slaughtered poultry: chickens and ducks. When I was a kid, most farmers around Montgomery raised chickens as we did. In spring they purchased day-old chicks from the hatchery in town and raised them in warm brooder houses. At 10 or 12 weeks of age, the chicks were well feathered and had learned to roost. Most of the cockerels (young males) were sold as fryers. The pullets (females less than a year old) were kept for egg laying.

In late spring we started butchering cockerels—those we raised as well as others we purchased from farmers. These "springers" sold well in the meat market. Throughout the year we butchered older laying hens that had been culled from flocks and replaced with young pullets. We butchered a few ducks, usually just during the holiday season.

Chickens to be butchered were kept in a small chicken coop behind the meat market. Most often we butchered on Saturday mornings so that dressed chickens would be available for sale during the weekend (roast chicken, dressing, with mashed potatoes and gravy was a popular Sunday dinner menu).

Killing chickens can be done in several ways. My wife Shirley was raised on a farm. When the farmers she knew butchered springers or wanted a hen for Sunday dinner, out came a hatchet or heavy knife and off came the chicken's head on a chopping block.

We killed chickens in the back room of the meat market. Our procedure went like this: First, we had to catch the chickens in the chicken coop—not an easy task. We used a stiff wire rod, about four feet long and curved into a hook at the end, to catch each chicken by the leg. About 15 or 20 chickens were caught in this way and put into crates made of wooden slats. One or two crates of chickens were dragged into the back room. A large chest-high wooden barrel with the bottom knocked out was rolled next to the crates.

Killing the chickens was best done by two men, although one man could manage. The first man reached into the chicken crate, through a sliding door, and grabbed a chicken—then handed it to the second man holding a boning knife with a pointed narrow blade (sharpened down to about ½ inch wide) and a straight cutting edge.

The man with the knife stood astride the bird and held the bird between his legs. With his free hand the man took the chickens' head and pulled, stretching the bird's neck. With the boning knife he stuck the chicken through the neck (just behind the head) and cut up against the neck bone and down until the blood gushed. Then with a simple twist of the wrist, the man broke the chicken's neck and tossed the bird into the barrel, flapping and jumping crazily as it bled out. In five to ten minutes, all the chickens were killed and the barrel filled. All in all, a very efficient system.

Handling the knife when killing chickens required some dexterity, and I found I was good at it. As fast as a helper handed me a chicken, it was grab, hold, stick, cut, twist, and toss—nearly in one fluid motion—and in a matter of seconds the bird was in the barrel. This part of butchering chickens I didn't mind, but the next, scalding and cleaning the birds, was just drudgery.

When the chickens in the barrel quit fluttering, the barrel was lifted and the birds came out the open bottom and onto a pile on the cement floor.

To "clean" or remove feathers from market poultry, we used wet plucking or scalding rather than dry plucking. To scald chickens, one man took two chickens by the feet and dunked them into a large bucket of hot water (about as hot as for scalding hogs) and swirled them around for about 25 seconds or so until the feathers could be picked off easily. Then the scalded chickens were laid on the wooden bench. The second man would take a scalded chicken by the legs and, by rubbing the bird by hand, peal off large clumps of feathers until the bird was clean.

Bending over a bench full of scalded chickens, particularly on a sweltering July afternoon, was not a picnic. But what bothered me the most was the rank smell of hot wet feathers. It's a smell hard to describe, because it is so singular, but by comparison I thought it second only to the stink of hog feces in being disagreeable.

After the chickens had been cleaned, they were cooled in a barrel of cold water. This plumped up the birds, making them more attractive and easier to "draw" or eviscerate.

The chickens were gutted and dressed for sale. Four or five chickens at a time were displayed on enamel trays in the refrigerated display case in the front room.

Looking back, I can't say killing livestock bothered me. As I grew up helping my father in the slaughterhouse, I assimilated his attitude and feelings about the trade. So completely had I adjusted to this work that I remember being amazed when two grade-school chums came out to watch us butcher a steer—and left at the first sight of blood, one even getting sick to his stomach.

There was one incident I recall, however, that did trouble me. It happened when I shot a horse. It was at a time when farmers were replacing their workhorses with tractors and selling the horses at cut rates. My father had purchased some horses to butcher as food for his dogs. We started slaughtering them in winter, one at a time as needed for the dogs, and hanging the quarters in the hide house. Since we didn't need to be careful about getting the meat dirty, we shot the horses in the corral and skinned them out there.

I had never shot a horse before and I did not feel comfortable. As I took the rifle and walked into the corral, I took notice of the big chestnut gelding trotting back and forth nervously, unsettled by the strange surroundings. He was in prime condition, I thought, still young enough to provide a decade or more of good service. It seemed a shame to kill him.

Soon the problem I had was getting the rugged workhorse to stand still and face me so I could shoot him in the forehead. I talked softly to the red gelding, trying to settle him down, but he seemed to grow more anxious, cantering around the corral and avoiding me as if he knew what was coming.

Finally the horse stopped and watched me from the corner of his eye, showing me his head in profile. I shouldered the .22 and leveled at the gelding's left eye; whispering the words "easy boy" in a gently litany until he turned his head and gave me the shot I wanted. But as I squeezed the trigger, the muscular horse jerked his head up and the bullet struck his muzzle, just below the eyes. The horse reared up and gave a sharp cry—like a child in pain—and fell back against the rail fence, his eyes wide in fear. As blood streamed from his nose, the gelding struggled to regain his footing. With trembling hands I quickly reloaded and fired again—this time a killing shot.

I remember helping my father skin the gelding, but I couldn't get the sight and sound of that killing out of my mind. I had missed a clean, first-shot kill before with cattle, but was never bothered like this. The reason: it was a horse.

For me horses were a step above other farm animals. They were loyal partners in farm work, they had personalities, they had names. Shooting a horse after it had given years of good service seemed a betrayal of trust. I never shot another horse.

My sensibility about slaughtering did eventually change, however, and for hunting as well. After my discharge from the Navy, I gave my rifle away. Several months later, my return to college marked the end of my days in the slaughterhouse. Now my wife and I feed deer, raccoons, birds, and just about every living creature that lives in the lake area behind our townhome. Shooting something now would sicken me.

15.

Baloney and Hot Dogs

THE KEY TO SUCCESS as a butcher in the old days was making good sausage. My grandfather knew this, having spent two years working in Herman Goehring's butcher shop in West St. Paul (starting at $10 per month) just to learn the skill before opening his own meat market in Montgomery in 1889. And when my father was in his late teens, Grandpa Conrad arranged for him to work a year or so for a sausage company in St. Paul to master the technique—and perhaps bring back some new ideas as well.

When I was growing up, my father was the sausage maker for the meat market. His bible was a battered, well-thumbed book with a red cover and Dad's name and address scrawled on the inside: *Secrets of Meat Curing and Sausage Making*. I found it in Dad's bedroom, after his death, tucked in the dresser drawer with his book on coonhounds and the photo album of his beloved hunting dogs.

The book was published in Chicago in 1929 by B. Heller and Company (Chemists), a supply company providing products for meat packers and butchers. It was a useful guide for a small town butcher, offering advice on such subjects as: killing and dressing meat animals, curing meat, sausage making, rendering lard, trimming and salting hides, and eliminating rats, flies, and cockroaches. The book listed 45 products and supplies that Heller's offered for sale, and included a one-page advertisement for each.

Although Heller's main products were various seasonings and curing ingredients for sausage, it also sold diverse products such as: the Butcher and Packer Thermometer, for controlling the water temperature in cooking sausage and scalding hogs; Tanaline, a tanning powder for all kinds of skins and pelts; the Slimeter, a hydrometer for gauging the strength of salt brine and curing pickles; and OZO Waste Pipe Opener, for dissolving scale and grease in stopped-up sinks, ice box pipes, and sewers.

For my father, however, the main section of the book contained recipes for 67 varieties of sausage, including such delicacies as Blood-Tongue Sausage, Kosher Mettwurst, Goose Liver Sausage, Fleischwurst (a German minced ham sausage), and Saxon Garlic Sausage (a knackwurst).

Because of a small customer base, my father had to limit the variety of sausages he made to the most popular: Bologna (ring) Sausage, Frankfurt Sausage, Liver Sausage, Headcheese, and Blood Sausage. Those varieties with limited appeal, such as Polish Sausage, Pork Sausage, Minced Ham Sausage, and Braunschweiger Liver Sausage, were purchased from Twin City packinghouses and delivered by refrigerator trucks.

Pork was the main ingredient of the liver sausage, headcheese and blood sausage—and just about every part of the hog that was not made into chops, roasts, and bacon went into it: The hog's head, including jowls, ears, and snout, went into the cooking kettle along with the tongue, skin, and tail.

When the meat was cooked and the spices added, it was ground very fine. Liver sausage and blood sausage were stuffed into casings and headcheese was stuffed by hand into clean and salted hog stomachs and sold by the slice.

The best sellers in our meat market were Bologna Sausage, commonly know as "baloney", and Frankfurt Sausage (wieners). The process and ingredients for making both were similar.

We made baloney and wieners about once a week, the amount depending on customer demand. Usually on Thursday we prepared the main ingredients: meat from bulls and cows—meat too tough or stringy for steaks and other choice cuts. My father rolled out several quarters of beef from the cooler, split them into huge chunks, and piled the pieces on one end of the long wooden table in the sausage room. Then with a boning knife, one man started "boning out" the meat (trimming the meat off the bones), piling the slabs of meat in the center of the table, and throwing the bones into a "bone barrel." With a butcher knife, the second man cut the slabs into golf ball sized pieces.

When the meat was cut up, it was spread out over the table, sprinkled with salt, cloves of fresh garlic, and Heller's brand Freeze-Em-Pickle cure, poured into a galvanized metal tub, and mixed thoroughly. If the meat was too lean, beef fat, and perhaps pork trimmings, were added to make the sausage "juicy." For wieners, my father added pieces of ham to provide a distinct flavor.

The tub of meat was placed on a sturdy wooden stool next to one of our two large, electric-motor-powered meat grinders. With both hands, a man fed meat into the mouth of the grinder, pushing the meat down into the revolving steel auger that forced the meat through the grinder's rotating knives and hole plate, and out the end into another tub.

Now the special seasoning and binder was put into the ground meat mixture. My father went to the "spice closet" and got a small pail full of Heller's Bull-Meat-Brand Flour, as a binder and absorbent, and a pound of Heller's Zanzibar-Brand Bologna Sausage Seasoning, to add the flavor of herbs and spices. (For wieners, Zanzibar-Brand Frankfurt Sausage seasoning was used). The flour and seasoning along with water were mixed into the tub of meat, and the meat put into the cooler to settle and cure until the next day.

The Heller's Zanzibar sausage seasonings came in various sizes: from as small as 10 pound cans to as large as 300 pound barrels. My father usually got the 25 or 50 pound cans. The colorful tin containers had pictures of tawny-skinned maidens with bare bosoms and dressed in sarongs carrying baskets of spices on their heads amongst swaying palm trees near a lush tropical lagoon. As a kid, I questioned why the girls wore so few clothes; then, as a teenager, with testosterone kicking in, my imagination took an entirely different slant.

On Friday morning the tub (or tubs if a bigger batch was to be made) of meat was taken out of the cooler and run through the meat grinder again—this time ground finer. The ground meat was poured into the heavy iron stuffer next to the sausage bench.

The sausage stuffer was shaped like a small cylindrical barrel with a hand-held crank attached. As the crank was turned, it pushed a large piston up and forced the sausage meat out a metal spout and into a casing.

The casings my father used to stuff sausage were the small intestines of cattle, hogs, or sheep that had been cleaned and salted. He purchased the 20 to 30 foot casings from meat packers—pressed flat, dry, and covered with salt—and shipped in wooden casks. Several hours before he used them, Dad soaked the casings in warm water to make them soft and pliable. Then he put one end of a long casing on the stuffer's spout, and worked it on as one works on the finger of a tight glove.

In making ring baloney, my father used a large spout and stuffed the sausage meat into 12 to 16 inch lengths. Another man tied the ends of the sausage links with string, forming a ring. With wieners, a slender spout was used and the entire length of the casing stuffed out and twisted into six-inch links. Then it was time for smoking.

Smoking meat gives it a special flavor, an appetizing color, and acts as a preservative. We smoked our baloney and wieners in a smokehouse just off the back room. The smokehouse was about 4½ feet wide and 15 feet long with brick walls and an iron beam running along each side at the ceiling.

To make smoke, Dad burned sticks of chopped hardwood (such as hickory, oak, ash, maple, and even apple tree prunings—with hickory and maple best for flavor) and sawdust.

Once there was sufficient smoke in the smokehouse, we carried in the baloney and wieners. For baloney, we ran a four-foot long smoke stick through a string of about 15 rings of sausage. Then we walked through a solid wall of smoke to the end of the smokehouse and hung each end of the stick of baloney on the iron beams. With wieners, we simply looped a whole string of links on the smoke stick and hung them across the beams. The baloney and wieners were kept in the smokehouse for several hours until they had a rich red color.

I was about 13 years old before I could hang sausage in the smokehouse. The iron beams were well over six feet off the floor, so you had to raise the stick of sausage over your head—making sure the stick was set correctly and would not fall down—all the while holding your breath to avoid a lung full of wood smoke. More than once I stumbled out of the smokehouse coughing, with tears running down my cheeks.

Once the baloney and wieners were smoked, it was time for the cooking kettle. We cooked our baloney and wieners in a large gas-burning kettle, about four feet in diameter, located in a small room between the smokehouse and the sausage room. Water was heated to about 160 degrees, and sticks of the sausages were taken right from the smokehouse and slid into the kettle. It took about a half hour for the ring baloney to cook (they were done when the rings floated to the surface) and 15 minutes for wieners.

When cooked, we hung the strings of baloney and bundles of wieners on racks and rinsed off the grease with boiling water; then submerged the steaming rings and links in cold water to shrink the casings and prevent shriveling. Next, we hung the sausages to dry before being placed in the walk-in cooler.

But eating baloney hot, right out of the cooking kettle, was a special treat. Mike and Adolph Kohout, from the Harness Shop, and some of the "boys" from the Palace Bar next door looked forward to sausage making day. Someone was always wandering into the sausage room asking, "Is the baloney ready yet?"

When the steaming rings of cooked baloney were lifted from the kettle, the word went out. Hungry men gathered in the sausage room and watched as my father tossed a hot swollen ring of sausage bouncing on the sausage table. He slipped a sheet of pink glazed butcher paper under the baloney, then with a boning knife, cut the ring into sections. At each slice, juice squirted out of the succulent meat and the spicy fragrance of garlic and herbs wafted up to trembling nostrils. As ravenous eyes watched, Dad stepped back and motioned to the men, saying, "Have a sample, boys."

As each man wolfed down a piece of sausage, my father piled a dozen or so rings of baloney on the table, knowing that to stop eating hot baloney after one small piece was like stopping after eating one potato chip.

The men knew the drill. If they wanted more sausage, they had to buy it. That meant taking the rings "up front" and having Miles "Lindy" Linberger, the front-room employee, weigh them. Usually a few regular patrons of the Palace Bar would each chip in a dollar or so and buy an armful of baloney, along with a loaf of white bread, and go "next door."

It was five steps from the front door of Bauer's Meat Market to the Palace Bar. Except for a few sundries, like potato chips and candy bars, the Palace did not sell food—yet more than a few meals were eaten there.

The saloon had four or five booths along one wall across from the bar. The men found an empty booth and opened the baloney and bread, laying the butcher paper across the tabletop. As one of the boys pulled out a pocketknife and cut the rings of baloney into pieces, another gent brought glasses of beer form the bar. They ate, daintily soaking slices of bread in the greasy juice that puddled on the waxy paper, and drank—quietly reveling in the "good life."

16.

Accidents

LEARNING THE TRADE included avoiding accidents. Farming, slaughtering, and sausage making were high-risk occupations involving dangerous machinery and unpredictable farm animals. But accidents could be prevented.

My father believed accidents were caused by carelessness, and that if you used common sense and paid attention to what you were doing, you had little to fear. He had no sympathy for the accident-prone, perhaps because he himself never had a work-related injury—at least none that I can recall.

I was different; I had accidents. The first "purple heart" I got in the line of duty happened while helping my father in the sausage room when I was about 12 years old. I was cutting meat with a butcher knife. We did not have metal mesh protective gloves in those days, and as I held the slab of beef with my left hand and cut with my right, I slashed my index finger to the bone. The cut laid back the flesh from the middle joint of the finger to the fingernail, with just a small flap of skin left to hold it to the finger.

As blood flowed off my hand, I went to Dad for guidance. With much work to be done, he was impatient and a bit angry at my negligence. "Go get a clean rag out of the spice closet and wrap your finger," he said, and kept on working. I did as I was told, stopping the bleeding by wrapping the finger and tying it with sausage string. When I got home, Mom put on a clean bandage.

Several days later I took a spill with my bike, got the wound dirty, and developed blood poisoning (infection). This sent me to Dr. Fred for treatment, and several days in bed before the infection cleared up.

Before I was 16 years old, I cut myself a second time on the same finger (much less serious), and took a bit of flesh off the end of my right thumb with the meat slicer. Whether these mishaps were due to carelessness, as my father thought, a lack of "focus", as they say now, or simply immaturity—I don't know. More likely it was a little of all three.

Conrad Bauer and Sons did have a good safety record, however. Except for myself, I can recall only one other employee accident— and it was terrible.

"Tommy" was one of several high school boys my father hired after I left and joined the Navy. One day Tommy, about age 17, was grinding meat in the sausage room while Dad was cutting meat on the sausage table.

In grinding meat, you had to first fill the mouth of the heavy grinder (about eight inches across), then push the chunks of meat down into the revolving steel auger to insure a smooth feed through the powerful motorized grinder's rotating knives and hole plate. Although my father had a wooden mallet for forcing the meat down, most of us simply used our fingers, hooking our thumbs under the rim of the grinder's gaping mouth to keep our hands from sliding into the auger. Other than our electric powered band saw, the two heavy-duty meat grinders were our most dangerous pieces of machinery.

As my father told the story, he was cutting meat, his back to Tommy as Tommy stood over the tub of meat feeding the grinder, when suddenly Dad was startled by a sharp cry of pain and terror.

He turned and saw Tommy slumped against the railing next to the grinder. His face ashen, Tommy was holding his left hand as blood poured from four bloody stumps where his fingers had been.

For a moment my father was stunned by the horror of it, then realized what had happened. Somehow Tommy's hand had slipped into the grinder; the powerful revolving auger had pulled his hand in and cleaved off all four fingers.

Dad rushed to Tommy's aid. He grabbed a butcher's apron and wrapped Tommy's hand to stem the blood flow, then took him down the street to the doctor's office and later to the hospital in New Prague.

My mother was called at home and hurried to the shop to help, bringing along my brother Milt. Lindy shared the appalling news. Tommy's parents were informed.

Years later, I talked to my brother Milt and Mom about the accident. Milt recalled that when it came time for cleanup, no one wanted to go near the grinder. Milt, then about 14 years old, got the job. With trepidation, he unscrewed the face cover and carefully removed the faceplate. As he pulled out the cutting knives, finger fragments—skin and bone—fell out. Unsettled, he gently lifted out the heavy screw-shaped auger. As he did so, a white bloodless finger dropped out. Shaken, Milt realized it was Tommy's index finger, remarkably whole and unmarked. Uncertain about what to do, Milt wrapped the finger in butcher paper and put it in his pocket.

Later in the day, Ben Kotek, part owner of the Palace Bar, came into the shop and heard about the finger. A Roman Catholic, Ben said the finger had to be given a decent burial, and said he would see to it. I heard later the finger was buried in a nearby cemetery.

My mother remembered that Tommy received cash and free tuition to business school from Employers Mutual Insurance of Wausau, our insurance company.

An ironical twist to this story is that some 20 years later, Tommy owned and operated the meat market for a year or so. How he managed with that injury I don't know.

17.

Meeting the Public

WAITING ON CUSTOMERS was the final step in learning the Bauer's butcher business. But before I was entrusted with that exalted position, I had to start with the front room basics: delivery and cleanup.

Each day after school, whenever I wasn't helping with farm work or butchering, I helped out at the shop. First I would check to see if there were any restaurant deliveries to make—we routinely delivered meat to several cafés in town. If yes, I walked the armful of packaged meat over.

Then came the wearisome job of cleanup. First, the electric power tools for cutting, sawing, and weighing had to be cleaned. With hot water and washrags, I would scrub off blood and particles of meat from the meat slicer, the tenderizer, and the scale. Then the inside of the band-saw cover had to be scraped clean of bone and meat "dust" and scoured.

Next came the butcher blocks. We had four thick wood butcher blocks for cutting and chopping meat and bone. By the end of the day, the tops of the blocks were covered with a greasy film of tallow and blood. We used a heavy wooden brush with metal teeth to rasp the blocks clean; sweeping debris onto the floor with a whiskbroom.

Then the sawdust-covered front room floor, soiled from the day's shuffling of customers' feet and the butcher block scrapings, was swept up.

Finally, greasy and blood-smeared butcher aprons were tossed into a box—to be picked up each week and laundered by an out-of-town cleaning company—and clean aprons hung up, ready for the next day.

In the late 1940s, when I was about 16 years old, I started my front room training in customer service. It began on a day when I did not have school: Saturday, the longest and busiest work day of the week. Bauer's Meat Market, like most stores on the main street, stayed open for business until 10 o'clock on Saturday nights. Since stores were not open on Sundays, Saturdays were big shopping days. Our Saturday, like every work morning, started at 7 a.m. My father and I met Lindy Linberger at the shop and "opened up" for customers.

We each had a job to do. My routine included cranking down the big canvas awning that protected our large plate glass front window from the early morning sun, spreading a thin layer of sawdust on the front room floor, and carrying out fresh vegetables from the walk-in cooler to fill the produce counter—carefully stripping off wilted leaves from the lettuce and cabbage and sprinkling the heads with water to give the appearance of freshness.

Lindy and Dad started sawing and cutting beef quarters and pork loins into steaks, chops, and roasts. These cuts of meat, along with a variety of cheeses, sausages, and luncheon meats, were laid on enamel trays and displayed in the refrigerated glass showcase. Stacks of ring baloney and a box of wieners on the counter next to the cash register let the vapors of garlic and spice entice impulse buying at check out. Glass jars of pickled pig feet were placed on the showcase at eye level to catch the fancy of workingmen looking for a quick lunch.

When all was in order, Lindy stayed in front to serve the trickle of early morning shoppers while Dad and I went to the back rooms to busy ourselves boning out beef quarters, grinding beef trimmings into hamburger, killing and dressing chickens, and so on. As the morning wore on, we kept an eye on customer flow up front and, if it got busy, Dad or I would help Lindy.

About midmorning, Lindy and I might make a small lunch of minced ham sandwiches, cupcakes, and coffee. My father wasn't much for eating snacks. At noon, Lindy went home for "dinner" and Dad stayed in front. When Lindy returned an hour later, Dad went home to eat and take a 20-minute nap (for Dad the nap seemed more important than the food). Sometime during those two hours I went home for a meal. In the afternoon, customer traffic picked up, and by early evening was at full throttle.

But it was on Saturday night (especially in summer) when Main Street was a tumult of activity. Farm families, after milking cows and doing chores, poured into town to shop and socialize. Farmers parked their cars, door against door, all along the "main drag"— rolling down windows to wave and visit with friends and neighbors that walked by on the sidewalk. The stores were jammed, and the Monty Theater had a full house of moviegoers for the big double feature. And from the seven bars and taverns in town, the sound of jukebox music and the shouts of laughter could be heard wafting out from doors kept open "to get air". Farm families strolled up and down the street, looking through well-lit show windows at women's dresses, men's overalls and work shoes, the kids begging for ice cream cones and candy.

In the meat market "all hands turned to"—even my mother came in to help. The front room was full of people milling around, some shopping, some visiting, and a farmer or two seeking out my father to dicker on a possible livestock sale. Sometimes a raccoon hunter would drop in to talk hunting, or to inquire about breeding his coonhound bitch to Dad's dog, Coke.

A frequent Saturday night visitor was Carl Ehmke, my father's fox-hunting partner. Carl, a Marlboro Man-handsome farmer in his late 30s, had a pack of fox-and-coonhounds like Dad and liked to talk hunting. He would come into the shop and take his usual place in the cutting room: leaning against a heavy cabinet covering the electric motor for our walk-in coolers.

Quiet and soft-spoken, Carl reminded me of an old-time cowboy. I watched with some admiration as he would casually tip his hat back, pull out a sack of Bull Durham tobacco from his shirt pocket and, with one hand, expertly roll a cigarette. Then with the cigarette dangling form his mouth and one eye half closed as smoke curled around his chiseled and deeply tanned face, Carl would lean back and watch the action around him—calmly waiting for a lull in customer activity so he could talk with Dad.

Saturday night finally ended sometime after 10 p.m. when the last customer ambled out and we finished cleaning up.

I learned important lessons in customer service: have a good product, deliver it in an appealing manner, and, above all, be dead honest in all your dealings.

As to product, I thought the quality of meat and groceries at Bauer's Meat Market was high—certainly according to small town standards at that time. And it was delivered in a pleasing manner. In that regard, Lindy Linberger set the bar very high.

I don't think you could find a better front man than Lindy. With his dark good looks, charming manner, and knowledge of each customer's likes and dislikes, he had a coterie of housewives who wanted his attention only. He knew all the many cuts of meat and would custom-cut each order—and if asked, offer advice for cooking each cut.

I tried to measure up to the standard Lindy set, but it was tough. I was friendly enough, but because I didn't work the front regularly, I did not have a good handle on customer preferences and price changes. Some customers were very fussy about how their beef or pork steaks and roasts were cut, and were quite disappointed when it was not done to their satisfaction. And there were always a few who expected you to know their preferences without having to be told. In this regard, I was not nearly as keen as Lindy.

And I still have nightmares about inadvertently overcharging a customer. For the products we sold, my father and Lindy decided on the selling price. For most of the cuts of meat in the showcase, Lindy stuck little plastic tags on each cut with the sale price per pound. Also, he kept a price list behind the counter near the scale for frequently requested items.

Sometimes, however, there were items left off the price list as well as not tagged; then, you had to remember the right price to charge. Usually when I could not recall the right price, I simply asked Lindy or Dad. However, there were times when I was alone in the shop (Lindy off to get a haircut and my father gone on some errand) and I had to make a decision on what to charge. In these situations I would charge a price lower than what it might be. I thought I'd rather error on the side of losing a profit than to "cheat" a customer.

And customers would know if you overcharged them. Some came in every day and often ordered the same item: a ½ pound of this cheese or a pound of that sausage, and so on. They were very price conscious and knew what Lindy had charged them in the past. Certainly they would ask Lindy or Dad if the price had changed. I thought if I charged less, they would simply accept their good fortune and remain silent. But if they found you had overcharged them, then you were either incompetent or dishonest. Either way, with three meat markets fighting for customers, this was a mistake you simply could not make. Fortunately, I never was accused of being dishonest or incompetent.

18

The Palace Bar—A Slice of Life

LEARNING THE TRADE exposed me to people from all walks of life. Our customers included those at the top of the socioeconomic pile: the banker, doctor, lawyer, clergy, and business leaders, on down to farm families, housewives of all income levels—and then the spillover from the Palace Bar.

A blue-collar drinking establishment, the Palace Bar made no pretense of class. Built about 1880, the two-story wood frame structure was a refuge for the workingman. Its weather-beaten store front on Main Street had a small plate-glass window—the only window in the bar—totally obscured by cardboard beer and whiskey signs, designed I am sure, to protect the patrons inside from inquiring eyes.

Walking into the Palace from off the street on a sunny day was like entering a different world. Your senses were quieted by the dim lamplight, the smell of tap beer and cigarette smoke, the soft murmur of men's voices, and the muffled shuffling of heavy work boots. To your left was a long oak bar with a brass foot rail and spittoons. A bartender in white shirt and apron served tap and bottled beer as well as spirits from the array of hard liquor bottles lined up on shelves behind the bar. On your right was a jukebox (rarely heard except on Saturday nights when farmers might bring in their wives and kids) and four or five booths. In the back was a small room piled high with cases of bottled beer.

The two owners of the Palace Bar, John and Ben, enjoyed a steady, dependable clientele. There were townsmen who came in once or twice a day for a "break". Whereas the white-collar businessmen, such as Curtis Westerman and Paul Ehrhard, executives of the Westerman's Lumber Company, and William Kozel, President of Citizen's State Bank, went to Della's Café for coffee breaks, some blue-collar tradesmen stopped at the Palace Bar, where they felt more comfortable, for the respite from work.

In the middle of most workday afternoons, you might see several shopkeepers in the Palace, there for a drink and a half hour or so of relaxation, as well as other men who came to the saloon whenever business brought them into town: farmers, livestock truckers, salesmen of one kind or another, providing a small but steady stream of customers. And then there were the half dozen or so men who made the Palace Bar their home.

I guess every small town has its characters; certainly Montgomery did. And whenever my brother Milt and I get together, the conversation becomes invariably a familiar recital of funny stories about several men who just about lived at the Palace Bar. In appearance they looked like men you'd have seen on a big city skid row years ago: grizzled and tough-looking, smelling of old sweat and wearing overalls that needed washing. Although hard drinkers, they were not bums; they worked, their hands rough and calloused from spade and pitchfork, digging graves or trenches for drainage tile, and helping farmers in need of an extra hand.

They were single men in their 30s and 40s with nicknames like "Doc" and "Carp". Some had no permanent address, choosing to bunk wherever they worked, sometimes staying at a flophouse in town called Brown's Hotel or simply sleeping wherever there was shelter from the elements. They came to the Palace Bar because it was one of the few places of business in town in which they were welcome.

Two of these men, Fattie and Ed, were buddies. It was a case of opposite attraction: Ed was friendly and outgoing and Fattie, suspicious and unsmiling. They had a beat-up 1938 Dodge parked behind the Palace Bar in which they slept. The wreck was not driven; it had no engine, but the car's seat cushions were soft. Fattie slept in the back seat and Ed in the front.

They came into the meat market often for meat and other groceries. My father hired them on occasion to help make hay or haul manure at the Slaughterhouse farm, sometimes giving them a job just so they could work off their meat bills.

Ed, short and stocky, spent a good share of his time digging graves in cemeteries in the Montgomery area. A moon-faced man with ruddy cheeks and a ready smile, Ed sometimes came into the shop when we opened at 7 a.m. to wait until the Palace Bar opened for business an hour later.

One July morning, just as we opened, Ed came into the shop all in a lather. "Christ almighty," he said. "I need a drink bad!" I asked him why and he told the story.

It had been stifling hot the last few days, and Ed had gotten up at sunrise to dig a grave. The grave he was digging was for a widow who had died the day before. She was being buried next to the grave of her husband, a huge, fat man who had died some time before.

The digging was going good Ed said, and he had gotten down the required six feet. Then to widen the grave, he thrust at the side of the hole with his sharp spade. The soft earth gave way, and his spade struck wood. It was the oversized casket of the widow's husband, and the blow had split it open. To Ed's horror, a putrid slime oozed out of the jagged hole in the casket's side.

As I write this, I remember how Ed struggled to explain how the scene assailed his senses. He did not have the facility with words as Edgar Allan Poe who, in his short story, *The Facts in the Case of M. Valdemar*, described the fluids of a rotting corpse as the "out-flowing of a yellowish ichor of a pungent and highly of-fensive odor" and again "a nearly liquid mass of loathsome—of detestable putrescence."

No, Ed was earthier. "Bart," he said. "It was yellow and green like pus; and the stink, worse than pig shit." Ed wrinkled his face in disgust and went on. "I liked to got sick to my stomach and I never threw up in my life." And that, knowing what Ed customarily ate and drank, made a powerful statement.

As Ed finished the story, the Palace Bar opened and Ed rushed over. He wanted to "get the smell out of his nose" with a drink or two, he said, adding that he'd probably buy a bottle to take along that evening to help him get through cleaning up the grave to make it ready for the widow's burial the next day.

Ed's partner was nicknamed Fattie, but it must have been a moniker hung on him as a child, for when I knew him he was rawboned. He walked hunched over with a rolling gait, his long arms and heavy hands swinging like a sailor who spent most of his years at sea. He wore bib overalls and a work shirt, the top button undone, showing tuffs of thick chest hair. His face, tanned and carrying heavy black stubble, was usually impassive, or, if upset, carried a scowl. I can't recall him ever saying hello on greeting or goodbye on departure.

Years of hard physical work with shovel and pitchfork had given Fattie powerful arms—and hands with a grip that could break another man's hand. It was said he had been near unbeatable as a younger man in a unique barroom contest that pitted two men: each facing the other across a table. Reaching across the table with an outstretched hand, they would lock middle fingers and pull—the winner being the man who pulled the other man's hand across a set line on the table, or forced him to release his finger grip.

I had only heard about these old-time contests, never having seen one myself, and asked Fattie one day about them and the secret of his prowess. He had come into the sausage room with a ring of baloney with plans to cut it up for lunch. For some reason, he was willing to talk.

"See this finger?" Fattie said, putting the knife down and stretching out his left had. I noticed the middle finger was curled in the shape of a hook. "You see," he went on, "I broke this finger one summer and didn't get to a doc. I kept working making hay, and the finger healed wrapped around a pitchfork."

"Well how does that help you in a table fight?" I asked.

Fattie chortled. "Once we lock fingers, the only way the other guy can get me to lose my grip is to break my finger and straighten it out—and that's never happened."

Fattie's eating habits would have made a dietitian cringe. He was a meat eater; the only fruit or vegetable I ever say him eat was raw onions and garlic.

Usually whoever hired Fattie fed him; and if it was a farmer, the farmer's wife made sure he ate good. But if he was between jobs or the weather was too bad to work, often Fattie came into the meat market to eat.

If we were making ring baloney or wieners, when we finished Fattie always asked for the couple of pounds of raw meat that remained in the stuffer. If it was not available, he'd buy several pounds of raw hamburger and cloves of fresh garlic, onions, and four or five eggs. Then he took the makings into the sausage room and laid it all on a sheet of butcher paper on the sausage table. He'd flatten out the meat into a huge patty, then peel the garlic and onions and chop it all into the meat. On top of this meat patty, he broke the eggs and mixed them in with a butcher knife, finally adding salt and pepper to taste. For a beverage, Fattie pulled out a half pint of Four Roses whiskey from a brown paper bag. There were always forks and spoons in our spice cabinet for his eating utensils.

Fattie ate and drank without conversation. When he finished, he wiped his mouth on his shirtsleeve and took a final swallow of whiskey, slipped the near empty bottle in his hip pocket, and swaggered out the back door. Later, I'd see Fattie's feet sticking out the open side door of his Dodge where, in the back seat, he was sleeping off the meal.

Fattie was a veteran, having been drafted into the U.S. Army during World War II, but he didn't serve long. He was discharged, it was said, in less than six months; some said it was a medical discharge, other that he was released as "unsuitable for military service." Whatever the reason, I could understand Fattie having trouble in any organization as structured and authoritarian as the Army. Along with his affinity for drink, he did not like anyone telling him what to do. And with such a prickly personality, Fattie probably had few friends.

But Fattie was proud of his army service. When drunk he would come weaving into the Palace Bar, his eyes wild and his face aflame. As he approached the line of men lounging at the bar, he'd straighten up, and with shoulders back shout out in a commanding voice, "T-Hut. Private E___ W___ reporting for duty—Sir!" Then he'd march to the bar and order, "Barkeep, bring a bottle."

And Fattie was just plain tough. He seemed indifferent to discomfort and pain. I remember coming to the back of the meat market one cold and blustery winter morning to open up. I noticed the door to our woodshed was half open. Snow was blowing into the woodshed and a small snowdrift had piled up around the door. I was irritated because I thought someone had neglected to shut the door properly the night before. As I shoveled the snow away, I looked into the woodshed and noticed a figure spread-eagled across the tumbled pile of wood. It was Fattie, without coat or cap, lying on his back with arms outstretched. Snow had drifted over and around him. His shirt was open, showing chest hair caked with snow. An empty bottle of whiskey lay at his side.

I rushed to Fattie, thinking he was dead. His eyes were closed, his body without life, but a perceptible vapor came from his open mouth. He was alive! I shook him awake. He mumbled something about whether the Palace Bar was open and said he was stiff and needed a drink. I told Fattie it was only seven o'clock and that he'd have to wait another hour, and then helped him into the shop to warm up.

As much as Fattie violated the rules of healthy living, he enjoyed one very important attribute—luck. Like a cat, he seemed to have had nine lives. I remember one warm Saturday night. It was about 10:30 and we had finished cleaning up after closing the shop at ten. I went through the Palace Bar and out to the back alley where our Chevy was parked behind our woodshed. Without a streetlight it was very dark, and as I groped around the car and opened the front door, my leg bumped an inert object. The hair on the back of my neck bristled. In the dim beam of the car's dome light, I looked down and saw a man's arm.

I reached into the glove compartment and fetched a flashlight. Carefully shining the light under the car, I confronted a man's face. It was Fattie, eyes closed, snoring softly, obviously dead drunk. His head lay right behind my left front tire. If I had not bumped into his arm and backed the car out, I would have driven over his head and neck.

On another occasion, Fattie's luck held, but not completely. It was night and he was drunk and passed out in the alley behind the Palace Bar. A car came through and, not seeing Fattie in time, drove over him, breaking both his legs. A sister who lived in a small house on the west side of town took Fattie in until he recovered and went back to work.

I was told that when Fattie and Ed got too old to work they moved into a small house outside of town. Although Fattie never fired a rifle in anger, his brief military service qualified him for veterans' benefits. I heard he died in his 60s in the Veterans Home near Hastings, Minnesota.

Another character who found the Palace Bar a comfort was Doc. Doc was one of several unmarried siblings who lived on a farm south of town. I remember as a kid going with my father to the Doc's farm to buy cattle. As we walked through the livestock barn, I was struck by the number of empty PM whiskey bottles scattered about in empty horse stalls and feeding troughs.

Doc didn't come to town often, but when he did everyone knew it. I don't believe Doc owned a car, so when he got a ride into town in the morning, he stayed until someone took him home—whether that be at night or the next day. A slender man with graying stubble on his face, Doc would walk up and down Main Street seemingly in a hurry, his eyes looking this way and that, as if searching for someone or something. Whether in July or December, he always wore bib overalls with the cuffs of his trouser legs rolled up several turns allowing one or two inches of his long johns to show.

It seemed Doc seldom had money, but always a big thirst. He would start at the Palace Bar looking for someone to buy him a drink. If unsuccessful there, he'd make the rounds of the other saloons, hoping to get lucky. He was not always welcome. When he came into the American Legion Club, the genial bartender would announce: "We don't need a doctor today—out!"

One story that went around had it that when Doc came into one joint, a patron with a sick sense of humor decided to play a trick. He took his glass of beer to the toilet, drank a few swallows, and then put a "head on it" with a generous urine sample. Doc was at the far end of the bar trying to mooch a drink when the trickster came out. He called Doc over and offered him the beer. Doc, unaware of the ruse, thanked him and quaffed it down. Doc wiped the foam off his upper lip with the back of his hand and thought for a minute. Then he looked at the bartender with an expert eye and pronounced: "Barkeep, you'd better check that barrel of beer you're tapping. I think it's gone bad."

I'm not sure how truthful that story was, but it sure got plenty of laughs.

Then there was the time Doc gave my parents quite a scare. It was a Saturday night and they had closed the shop, come home, and gone to bed. Our bedrooms were all upstairs. Milt and I, being little at the time, slept in bunk beds in one room with the door closed. Mom and Dad slept in a bed at the top of the stairs.

It was about 1:30 in the morning when my mother heard a noise in the kitchen downstairs. Frightened, she shook my father awake. They listened. Someone was moving around. In the dark Dad fumbled around for some kind of weapon before confronting the intruder. The only thing available was one of Mom's high-heeled shoes. So down the stairs Dad crept, a high-heeled shoe in one hand, adrenaline pumping—having no idea who or what to expect. The light switch to the kitchen was at the foot of the stairs. Dad clicked on the light and stood ready to fight. There, sitting in a chair at the dinner table was Doc—drunk. "Milt," Doc mumbled, "can you loan me a quarter?"

Recently Mom told Milt and me that, like most people in town in those days, we never felt the need to lock our doors. Doc had simply walked into the house. She said Dad was so angry he ordered Doc out. Since it was summer, Doc probably slept it off in the apple orchard behind our house.

In the years that followed, I lost track of Doc. Then in April 1994, my father entered the Mala Strana Health Care Center in New Prague. Dad was 90 years old and in need of skilled nursing care for advanced pulmonary fibrosis. The nursing home assigned two patients to a room. As we took Dad by wheelchair into his designated room, I glanced at the terribly old and wizened little man curled in a fetal position sleeping in the next bed—my father's new roommate. I didn't recognize the old man and asked the young nurse for particulars. She said he was 93 years old and had lived for years in a board and care home in Montgomery until he became totally incontinent and in need of a skilled nursing home. It was Doc!

The irony of the situation was not lost on Dad. He shook his head sadly at the strange quirk of fate that brought him and Doc together to face their last days.

While visiting my father during the next few weeks, I noticed Doc rarely talked, seemed indifferent to his surroundings, and spent most of his time sleeping. Occasionally he would shout out for an aide when his urine bag was full.

Then one day a month or so later, I came into my father's room and noticed Doc's bed was empty. Dad said Doc died the day before. He said an aide brought Doc back to their room after lunch in the cafeteria. Doc lay down to nap. Soon after, Doc got sick and vomited on the floor. Dad called for help. When the aides came, they found Doc dead, apparently from a heart attack.

There were other characters like Fattie and Doc that walked through the Palace Bar doors 60 years ago. I wonder if men are made like that anymore.

19.

Death Throws a Punch

DURING THE 1930s, Grandpa Conrad (in his 60s and in declining health) turned over the active operation of Conrad Bauer and Sons to Uncle Bill and Dad. Over the years, grandfather had built a well-diversified business extending beyond the meat market (farm land, real estate, etc.) that was debt free. It was well positioned to survive the Great Depression, and did.

Then came World War II. For retail meat markets it meant rationing and price regulation. Washington rationed scarce commodities like meat, sugar, gasoline, and tires, and kept prices from increasing. The effect on Conrad Bauer & Sons should have been a flattening of gross sales—but that's not what happened. The reason: a major contract with Minnesota Valley Canning.

MVC was canning sweet corn and peas to feed the armed forces, as well as the home front. It had canning factories in six small Minnesota farm communities: LeSueur (the company's home office), Cokato, Blue Earth, Winsted, Watertown, and Montgomery. During the summer canning season, the factories often operated around the clock. Local people, young and old, men and women, college and older high school students, all took jobs in the canning factories. Mexicans and even German war prisoners (in Montgomery) handpicked the sweet corn.

The canning factories' work force needed to eat. Each factory had a canteen where meals were served. Bauer's Meat Market had for years supplied meat to the Montgomery plant. But now Minnesota Valley was asked to increase production. They sought a contract with one meat supplier for all its plants, and contacted Conrad Bauer & Sons.

Bauers was anxious to contract with Minnesota Valley, and assured the canning company it could supply all the meat it needed. But there was a major problem. Bauers needed authorization from the federal government in the form of a special license.

Working through government machinery to get a license was slow and cumbersome. And what clout would a small town meat market have in the Roosevelt administration, especially when its founder, Conrad Bauer, was a staunch Republican? But this was wartime, and decisions regarding the war effort were being made in the nation's capital.

Then MVC stepped in. Edward B. (Ward) Cosgrove, its CEO, flew to Washington and got things done. On October 18, 1943, Conrad Bauer & Sons was issued a license as a Class Two Slaughterer by the War Food Administration of the Federal Government— acting under the Second War Powers Act of 1942. This license authorized Conrad Bauer & Sons to "conduct operations in accordance with all orders of the War Food Administration issued for the purpose of distributing meat in the interest of effective prosecution of the war."

With this license, Bauers entered into an exclusive contract with Minnesota Valley to supply all its meat—and for Conrad Bauer & Sons the contract was lucrative. Meat rationing and price controls did not affect this part of the business. Gross sales soared.

And the workload jumped. Now, instead of slaughtering the usual two or three cattle a week, Dad was butchering one or two cattle a day! The work was hard, but the booming war years were exhilarating. Too old to be drafted into the Armed Forces, Dad and Uncle Bill could still do their part in the war effort, and do good business. They even bought stock in the Minnesota Valley Canning Company.

Now after 50 years in business, Conrad Bauer & Sons was at its zenith. Profits were the highest ever, and the future looked bright. Then, an unexpected turn of events almost finished the firm.

On the night of November 11, 1945, while coon hunting, Uncle Bill fell down a small ravine and broke his leg. Not a serious fracture, and with his life-long good health, Bill's convalescence was expected to be brief. But healing was unnaturally slow. Bill, unable to work in the shop, spent the fall and winter at home with his side business: buying furs (mink, muskrat, and weasel) from local trappers for sale to furriers in St. Paul.

In late winter, Bill developed a slight throat infection. With the leg not healing and a nagging painful throat, Bill and family members were concerned. Dr. Fred Westerman, uncertain about the problem, thought Bill's teeth might be bad and referred him to a dentist. A dental examination found Uncle Bill's teeth to be sound. Finally in April of 1946, referral was made to specialists in St. Paul. The diagnosis was bad: carcinoma of the thyroid.

On April 29, 1946, Uncle Bill was hospitalized at Abbott Hospital in Minneapolis and began radiation therapy. With his swollen throat burned dark from repeated X rays, Bill struggled against the unrelenting malignancy, but the cancer's spread could not be stopped. His body withered and dropped below 100 pounds, but Bill with his strong heart and optimism kept up the fight.

With the end near, Dr. Schaff, the attending physician, advised the family that Uncle Bill could not survive and had to be told. No one stepped forward, all afraid to be the bearer of such terrible news. Finally Dr. Schaff approached my father. "Milt, you are his brother. You must tell him now."

My father often said how hard it was to do. For weeks Bill had been making plans for the future, plans that involved Dad in expanding the business. It was always "when I'm out of the hospital we will do this," or "when I'm back on my feet and in the shop we will do that."

To make it more poignant, after years of rivalry and emotional distance, Bill reached out to Dad to close the gap: to be buddies again as they were when young. "When I'm well," Bill urged, "we will have a big vegetable garden—just like when we were kids. We will work it together."

But the day came. Bill, eyes sunken, voice a hoarse whisper, once again talked of coming home and plans for the future. Father knew the time was at hand. Pulling his chair close to Bill's hospital bed, he said, "Bill, you won't be coming home. Dr. Schaff said they can't cure your cancer." Bill stared into my father's face, looked into his eyes—said nothing.

Father continued, "Dr. Schaff wanted you to know—so you could settle your affairs." Bill turned his head away, closed his eyes—silent. Uncle Bill died several days later on August 22, 1946.

"When I told him he was not going to get well, he believed me," Dad said. "He knew I would never lie to him. We might argue and disagree on things, but we never lied to one another."

The obituary headline, in bold letters on the front page of the Montgomery Messenger, announced: "THRONG ATTENDED W. BAUER FUNERAL" and "The Rev. Conrad J. Buehler Officiated at Last Rites for Prominent Young Man at St. John Lutheran Church Last Saturday Afternoon."

The Messenger went on to describe his work, interests, hobbies, and generosity: "Bill was one of the well known young men of this community, having entered his father's business in his early teens and being in daily contact with people in all walks of life, in that he spent most of his time behind the counter in the meat market until he was taken ill. It is generally known that during that long period of years he was credited with many kind acts of charity among the people really in need. He had confidence in his home community and invested a greater part of his earnings in farm property in the locality."

I remember well Uncle Bill's wake. Lines of people waited in the warm August evening to enter the family home and file past the bier, to get one last look at the energetic and sociable butcher they knew so well. Folding chairs on the lawn outside were filled with business friends and rivals, farmers and fellow sports fans, and long-time customers of the shop—paying their respects. The Messenger summed up the feeling: "In all he was a general good fellow and his presence in the community, where he spent his entire life, will be missed." In a small town that is about as good a tribute as a man can get.

Although I was only 13 years old when Uncle Bill died, my feelings about him were like most folks: he was a good guy. He was kind to me and on several occasions took me fishing.

Uncle Bill's incapacity during the winter of 1945 and spring of 1946 cast a dark shadow over the fortunes of Conrad Bauer & Sons. Then as it became apparent that Bill would not get well, a deep gloom enveloped the Bauer families. Grandfather, now in his 80s and with diminished physical and mental capacities, was unable to help make the vital decisions necessary to keep the firm afloat. Father, exhausted from the heavy slaughtering demand of the Minnesota Valley contract, could not absorb Bill's front office and customer work.

What to do?

Then two young employees of the firm, Lindy Linberger and Emil Mucha, stepped forward with an offer. Would Conrad Bauer & Sons lease the business to them for one year? They wanted to take a shot at running it.

The proposal was audacious but not farfetched. They had experience. Both started work for Bauers as teenagers before the war:

Lindy working for Uncle Bill serving customers in the shop, and Emil working for father in the slaughterhouse and sausage making operation. They entered the military during the war and now, in their early 20s and the war over, both were back and working full time.

During Uncle Bill's incapacity, Lindy, a dark, handsome man with a friendly personality, moved easily into the vacuum and displayed a talent for customer service. Emil, of Bohemian descent, short and barrel-chested with an exuberant personality and willingness to work hard, showed he deserved a chance to fill Dad's shoes.

A deal was struck. In June of 1946, Conrad Bauer & Sons leased the business to Messrs. Linberger and Mucha for one year with the understanding that father would continue as consultant and receive $200 a month.

During the year of the lease, Lindy and Emil worked hard and the business held its own, but the partnership showed strain. Father, in turn, having recovered from Uncle Bill's death and grown restless with inactivity, was not entirely satisfied with the firm's management.

Toward the end of the lease, during the summer of 1947, father decided to take mother, Milt Jr., and me on a six-month trip by car to the western states. It was the first time we as a family had gone anywhere on a vacation—and it turned out to be a wonderful adventure. And it gave Dad a chance to think: of the business and his future.

On our return, father was rested and exhilarated. Only 44 years old and in his prime, he wanted the business back. With agreement from all parties, the lease was not renewed. Lindy kept his job and went on salary. Emil decided to leave and took employment as manager of the meat department for the Piggly Wiggly supermarket (a large chain store) in Faribault, MN.

Before Uncle Bill's death, arrangements were made for him and my father to buy out Aunt Esther and Dorothy's interest in the meat market, feeding farm, and slaughtering operation.

Following Grandfather's death on June 4, 1948, the business, Bauer's Meat Market, was owned by my father and Anna Bauer, Uncle Bill's widow—a 50/50 partnership.

But Dad chafed under this arrangement. If he was solely responsible for working the business, he wanted to own it.

In 1950, father approached Anna with an offer. Would she sell her interest in the business to him? If she refused, he would sell his interest to her. He wanted 100% of the business—or none.

Anna was interested in selling and a deal was made. Now Dad was the sole owner of Bauer's Meat Market.

V. A CHANGE *in* DIRECTION

20.

Trying to Be Someone

IN SEPTEMBER 1946, my world changed. At age 13, I began my freshman year at Montgomery High School.

Going from 8th grade to high school was a big step, and like most freshmen, I tried hard to fit in, to be somebody. For boys, being an athlete was the way to get recognition, both from other boys and certainly from the girls. The town boys I knew were shooting baskets and playing baseball. They knew nothing about coon and fox hunting and cared less. Their goal was to make varsity in high school sports. That became my goal too.

Monty High had three sports: football, basketball, and baseball. I had never played basketball or baseball, but I thought I might have a chance in football. I told my father I was going to try out. He didn't say much, but I could tell it didn't sit well with him. Dad had not gone to high school and had never played team sports. For him it was a waste of time.

I went to football tryouts, but it was tough. I was small and weighed less than 110 pounds. I didn't get a uniform, but the coach kept me on the practice squad, one of the "scrubs."

I was determined though. And by my junior year I weighed about 140 pounds—lean and well muscled from farm work. I discovered I could block and tackle well. I made starting guard on offense and defensive back on defense. I had arrived!

I was committed to high school. I got into acting and had important roles in several class plays. I was elected president of the "M" Club—the varsity lettermen's club.

As my interest in school activities grew, I lost interest in hunting with my father. I found excuses not to go.

In time an emotional distance developed between Dad and me. He never asked me about schoolwork or high school activities; never went to any of my football games or plays. And because Dad didn't go, Mom did not go either. Because in those days, it was considered unseemly for a wife to go out at night alone without her husband.

A smoldering tension, barely contained, grew between my father and me. Then one day, Dad's feelings exploded. "Why aren't you like Lee D.?" Dad asked. There was pain and discouragement in his voice.

Lee D. was a farm boy who started freshman year with me but had quit school at age 16. Lee loved coon hunting and had coon dogs. He would come to the shop and ask my father's advice about hunting and share coon hunting stories.

Dad's outburst made it clear to me: I had failed him. He wanted a boy like Lee. I could never be my father's son.

But there was one person in town who believed in me: the Reverend Albert H. Guetzlaff, the pastor of St. John Lutheran Church in Montgomery—my church.

Rev. Guetzlaff came to Montgomery as the church minister about 1948 after serving Lutheran pastorates in South Dakota, Iowa, and Minnesota. A well-built man in his early 30s and sporting an athletic crew cut, Pastor Guetzlaff took a special interest in me. He encouraged my participation in church activities. I was active in Luther League and through his influence became president. In summer I attended Lutheran Bible Camp near Onamia and Mille Lacs Lake. In time I tried my hand teaching Sunday school, singing in the choir, and ushering.

Pastor Guetzlaff began talking to me about going to college—specifically Wartburg College in Waverly, Iowa. He had received a B.A. degree from Wartburg in 1937, and a diploma in theology from the Wartburg Theological Seminary in 1940. He talked about the excitement of college life, and the possibility of playing football and acting in plays. Although he did not say he wanted me to go to Wartburg to become a minister, clearly that was his intent. Years later he wrote me and said, "I had you pegged to become a pastor. That's why I attempted to have you attend Wartburg." And to top it off, he arranged a Wartburg College parish scholarship of $200 at $50 per year to go to Wartburg.

I talked to my parents about going to college. Dad said little and Mom less. Once I agreed to go, things happened fast. I applied to Wartburg and was accepted. My high school coach put in a good word for me with the Wartburg football coach. Soon I got word to report to the Wartburg campus the following August for football tryouts. During the summer of 1950, I tried to gain weight and strength for college football. Farm work helped, and by August I weighed 150 pounds and felt strong.

I was apprehensive when Dad, Mom, and I drove south to the river town of Waverly, Iowa, 22 miles north of Waterloo with a population of about 6,000. I didn't know anyone at the college and wondered what was in store for me. The campus was deserted when we arrived, as classes were not to start until the middle of September. Along with other football hopefuls, I checked into Grossman Hall, the men's dormitory.

After a week or so of orientation and conditioning exercises, Coach Melvin "Nellie" Nelson got the linemen together and started one-on-one drills. As a group, the college players were better than in high school, but I was holding my own. My college football career, however, was to come to an abrupt end.

One day I was working against a big lineman in drill. He knocked me off balance and came down hard on my foot. I felt a sharp pain and hobbled off the field. I had a hairline fracture just above my big toe. For the next few days I watched practice from the sidelines. Then I put on the pads and tried working out. It was no go. I couldn't push off on that foot without pain.

Although discouraged by sitting out practice, I was realistic. I watched as Coach Nelson selected his first and second teams. Even after I recovered I could see I wasn't big enough to play the line, and I didn't think the coach would use me in the secondary. And most importantly, the thrill I got playing high school football was gone.

Just before classes started, I went to the coach and said I was quitting football. He wasn't pleased, but I think he understood. (As it turned out, the season was not good. Racked with injuries all year, the football team won just one game.)

Now that I was off the football team, I had to find another place to live. Upperclassmen had first dibs on Grossman Hall so I had to look off campus. I found a basement apartment with two other students in a big two-story house about eight blocks from the college. To help pay my rent, the owner, a Dr. Sparks, paid me 75 cents an hour for doing odd jobs around the house: raking the lawn, washing and putting on storm windows, etc. During the week I ate meals at the dining hall on campus, and on weekends lived on cheeseburgers at a greasy-spoon diner near the house.

On September 15, 1950, 212 other freshmen and I began our first year of studies at Wartburg College. An American Lutheran liberal arts school, Wartburg was founded in 1852. It got its name from the castle of Wartburg in Saxony where Martin Luther, the leader of the Protestant Reformation in Germany, hid after being excommunicated by the Roman Catholic Church. And it was where Luther began translating the New Testament into German. Many of the male students went to Wartburg to gain an undergraduate foundation for entry into a Lutheran seminary and, eventually, ordination as a Lutheran minister. Many girls studied for careers in teaching, or took parish education to prepare for church work.

It wasn't long after I selected courses and got my class assignments that I realized this was not to be like high school. I was overwhelmed with the amount of homework required. A language was necessary for graduation so I took German, thinking it would be easy. The professor was Frau Anna Elsa Jacob, a stickler on correct German grammar. For me it was incomprehensible. Soon I was on the verge of failing the course.

I was frightened of failure at Wartburg. Now that I was in college, Dad seemed resigned to the fact that I would not follow him into the butcher business—there was always my younger brother Milt to succeed him, and it might be a good thing to have a minister in the family. Dad put money in a checking account in the Citizen's State Bank and gave me a checkbook. I could not fail now.

I became a bookworm. I was sharing the one-room basement apartment with two other students. When the autumn chill came, the basement was cold and damp. A large furnace room was just off our basement living quarters. At night when my roommates went to bed, I went into the furnace room, wrapped myself in a blanket, sat next to the furnace to keep warm, and studied under the single light bulb that hung on a cord from the ceiling.

My diligent study habits did pay off. I got A grades in history and zoology and managed to pass German with a D plus, the lowest grade I ever got in college.

Wartburg was not all drudgery, though. I found time to join three student activities: the Wartburg Players, KWAR—the college radio station, and the Science Club.

Perhaps the most popular student organization on campus was the Wartburg Players, the dramatics club. More than 70 students, from a total student body of about 600, vied for the chance to perform on stage. Hoping to recapture the thrill I got acting in high school plays, I was quick to join.

The Wartburg Players had five shows scheduled for the 1950–51 year—all to be held in the Little Theater, a small one-story building with an elevated stage and high ceilings. The first play of the season was "Elizabeth the Queen." I tried out for any part and ended up with the most insignificant one in the show: the palace guard. Recently I looked through the FORTRESS, Wartburg College's yearbook for 1951. I found photos of three scenes from that production. I was pictured in each scene, dressed in slashed and puffed breeches and silk stockings, standing stiffly, an upraised spear in one hand, guarding the entrance to the Queen's chamber. I think the only words I said were something like, "You may not enter!"

I did not have a part in the next show, Dickens' "A Christmas Carol," but got a significant role in "Noah," the story of the Bible character and his family during the Flood, our Lenten production. I was cast as one of Noah's three sons (Sem, Ham, and Japheth), I can't remember which. I had one big scene. After 40 days and 40 nights of rain and darkness, I came out of the ark to see sunshine. I kept shouting: "The sun, the sun," over and over.

Our fourth show was a folk opera, "Down in the Valley," a musical set in some backwoods sleepy hollow. I was cast as "Pa," the father of one of the young lovers. I spent most of my time on stage talking slow and rocking in a rocking chair. That play did not get a good review in the Trumpet, our college weekly newspaper, but I was named as giving a worthy performance.

I did not have a part in our last play, "The Gorilla."

At the end of the dramatics season, I received an honor: nomination to Alpha Psi Omega, the national honorary dramatics fraternity. The Wartburg chapter of the fraternity was Lambda Mu Cast, and only a select group of seven dramatics students together with two faculty advisors held membership. Along with me were one or two other nominees. The Cast officers told us that before we could become members, we had to submit to an initiation ceremony. We were told little about the ceremony other than it would be held at night in the Little Theater, and that we each would have to act out a part from a play. Each nominee was given a different part to memorize. Mine was Mark Antony's oration at Caesar's funeral in Shakespeare's play, "Julius Caesar," which begins:

Friends, Romans, countrymen, lend me your ears.
I come to bury Caesar, not to praise him.
The evil that men do lives after them;
The good is oft interred with their bones.

On the night of the ceremony, I came early and sat alone in the darkened theater. The curtain on the stage was down. I was anxious, and in my mind I kept rehearsing the words of Mark Antony's soliloquy.

At the appointed time, the other nominees and I were taken backstage. In the blackness, our eyes were drawn to a single velvet-covered table lit by two flickering candles. Behind the table were three hooded figures in black robes. We were ordered to approach the table.

I stood at attention, head erect, arms pressed against my sides as a robed personage began a liturgical ritual—speaking of the sanctity of Alpha Psi Omega and the Wartburg Cast. Fear grew. We were questioned about dedication and loyalty and whether we possibly could be worthy of membership. I felt like a heretic on trial before a tribunal of the Spanish Inquisition.

Now came the final hurdle, the ultimate test of a thespian—can you act? Each nominee was asked to give the assigned dramatic presentation. When my turn came, I was struck dumb. I opened my mouth, but nothing came. All eyes were on me. The next thing I knew, I was on the floor with people around me.

I had fainted—the emotional distress overwhelming. In a few minutes I was all right, but the humiliation hurt.

I had no answer for what happened. I never fainted before. (Later, when I joined the Navy, I learned how to stand at attention. You stand straight, but not stiff—that can cut off blood circulation to the brain and you pass out. (I saw that happen to a few sailors in boot camp when, while standing at attention in formation on a hot asphalt parade ground during a lengthy inspection, they fell flat out—and no one was allowed to break ranks and help them.)

Everyone was sympathetic. Even though I failed the initiation test, I was accepted as a member of Lambda Mu Cast. Professor of English, Miss Erna Moehl, and a Cast advisor, wrote in my

FORTRESS:
Bart. It was wonderful having you join our midst this year. No one could have been more worthy. I always knew that I could count on you to the utmost. Yours is a friendship I hold very high. See you next year. Your friend, Erna.

Another student activity I tried was as a disc jockey on the college radio station KWAR, transmitted from a small room backstage in the Little Theater. The students had fun playing around with a variety of programs.

I had a half-hour show called "Rockin in Rhythm." My theme song was "Mr. Anthony's Boogie" by Ray Anthony. I played the favorite songs of the day and tried to include a few interesting comments. I soon discovered I didn't have the "gift of gab" to be a good DJ. I think the only response I got from the listening audience was a single postcard. It offered sympathetic encouragement.

With my focus on study, acting, and the radio station, I had little time for a social life; not that there was much of a social life to be had. About the swingiest place on campus was the Den, a little coffee shop downstairs in Wartburg Hall, the women's dormitory, where a boy could share lunch or coffee with a girl and listen to the jukebox. Consequently, I never had a date at Wartburg.

About the best I could do was to carry on a rich fantasy life. I had a secret crush on Myrna D., an attractive dark-haired sophomore cheerleader. She did not share my feelings, but was kind. In a beautiful hand she wrote in my <u>FORTRESS</u>: "Bart ... it was nice to make your acquaintance. Congratulation for the good work you did in Wartburg Players. See you around next year. Best wishes. Myrna."

As my first year of college came to an end, there was increasing concern about the war in Korea. After initial Allied success against North Korea, Red China unexpectedly entered the conflict. On November 25, 1950, Red Chinese troops swarmed across the Yalu River from Manchuria and, in savage fighting, split the thin Allied forces.

Early in 1951, General Douglas MacArthur, the supreme commander in the Far East, called for a strike directly at China in an effort to win a quick victory, President Harry S. Truman called him "out of sympathy" with U.S. policy and, on April 11, 1951, relieved him of all commands. MacArthur and his family made a triumphal return to the United States.

On April 19, 1951, General MacArthur was scheduled to address both houses of the U. S. Congress. It would be broadcast nationally on radio and television. My English professor, Mrs. A. E. Haefner, had the class listen to the radio broadcast saying "the general is a master of the English language."

Speaking eloquently and with intense sentiment, Gen. MacArthur gave his official farewell that day to the American people. The old warrior recounted his 52 years of military service and closed the historic speech with a quote from the old British barrack-room ballad: "Old soldiers never die," he said, "they just fade away."

The war was getting closer to home. I was hearing of high school buddies being drafted or enlisting in service. A few Wartburg students, although deferred, were, in patriotic fervor, quitting school and joining up. For me, it hadn't become an issue—yet.

During the fall of 1951, I decided I wasn't going to be a minister. The thought of taking Greek and Hebrew, the language requirements, was frightening. And I just didn't think I'd do well giving sermons.

The next question: If not the ministry, what then? In those days, if you asked the man on the street in Montgomery he'd say there were only two other professions worth pursuing—medicine and law. I could not see myself as a doctor.

I talked to my Aunt Esther Bauer about transferring to Macalester College and taking pre-law. She encouraged me.

My faculty advisor at Wartburg was Professor E. W. Hertel. I had taken Zoology and Botany from him and gotten A grades. He said I was a good student and tried to talk me into staying. I said my mind was made up. At the end of the first semester, I transferred to Macalester College in St. Paul.

Aunt Esther and Dorothy's house was adjacent to Macalester College. They had a basement apartment, but it was rented out for the year to other Mac students. Across the street, however, were a number of Quonset huts that the college built for married World War II veterans attending Macalester. There were some empty units for single students. I found a vacancy and shared a room with a Chinese student, Peng Chen.

Now that I was taking pre-law, I focused on political science and economics. I joined the Young Republican Club on campus. The year 1952 was an election year and the Republican Party had two strong candidates: former General Dwight D. Eisenhower and Senator Robert Taft of Ohio. The Young Republicans were split in their preference and there were spirited debates. Not knowing much about politics, I went with the popular favorite, Gen. Ike.

But by the end of my sophomore year, I was having second

thoughts about the field of law—and even about continuing college. Now that I was living in St. Paul, I was getting home some weekends and helping out in the meat market. Customers and friends advised me to quit college and go into business with my father. They said by not doing so I was throwing away a great opportunity of someday having my own business.

Then there was the guilt. Almost all my friends were in the service and several were fighting in Korea. One boy from Montgomery had been killed and another wounded. I was having trouble looking their parents in the face. One of my football teammates was fighting in Korea and got the Bronze Star Medal for gallantry. His father came into the shop and asked me when I was going into the service to do my duty. Being labeled a "draft dodger" in a small town was a terrible thing.

21.

Wearing the Navy Blue

DURING THE SUMMER of 1952, I struggled with conflicting feelings about my future. My Aunt Esther advised with passion that I stay in college. If I must enter the military, she said, I could take ROTC and go in as a commissioned officer. I talked to veterans of World War II and people I respected. Finally, I decided. I would enlist in the Navy and, after serving my country, go into the family business with Dad.

In August I drove to Mankato where there was a U.S. Navy Recruiting Office. Mom wanted to go along and I agreed as long as she didn't go into the office with me. The navy recruiter said with my two years of college I could go into the air arm of the Navy and get specialized training in service schools. The enlistment would be for four years. I signed up. A few weeks later I went to Minneapolis and, on September 10, 1952, took the oath and was sworn in.

The next step was recruit training at the naval training center in San Diego, California—"boot camp." I was one of a group of about 28 recruits, mostly from northern Minnesota, that went by train to San Diego. A navy bus met us and took us to the training center. As we passed through the gate, sailors waved and shouted, "You'll be sorry!"

It was my first inkling that my world was to change. I soon learned I was no longer an individual—I was part of a group, a company of about 120 men. Wherever we went—to the mess hall, to classes, washing our clothes—it was in formation.

Our first navy meal was breakfast. We were lined up and given trays. As we passed the steam tables, servers loaded our trays with an assortment of pork chops, pancakes, fried potatoes, eggs and more—not asking what or how much we wanted. Since as a boy I was taught to clean my plate, I ate everything. I went into boot camp weighing 150 pounds and came out three months later at 178 pounds.

One of the first things we learned was how to stand at attention and how to salute. To make sure we realized how insignificant we were, the chief petty officer in charge told us to salute "everything that moves or isn't nailed down."

The toughest thing for some in boot camp was the bag inspection. Each article of clothing had to be spotless, and marked, folded, and rolled in a specific way. On the day of inspection, each recruit had to lay out all his clothes in a precise manner for the Chief or inspecting officers to review. The slightest deviation meant a loss of points.

Our Chief, a salty old boatswain's mate, was a stickler during inspections and would at times use coarse language to set us straight. I remember him grabbing one recruit's rolled-up trousers and banging the soft and limp tube against the metal frame of the bunk. "This is pathetic," he growled in his harsh cigarette voice. "I want this rolled tight—so it's as stiff as a young man's pecker on his wedding night!"

After about eight weeks, we were allowed to leave the base for the first time. The Navy knew from long experience that young recruits getting their first taste of freedom after weeks of confinement on base would be apt to get into trouble. We were shown filmstrips depicting the ravages of syphilis and gonorrhea, and advised not to go across the border into Tijuana, Mexico. Tattooing, we were told, could be dangerous and lead to blood stream infection or hepatitis, and could result in a crude design we'd be stuck with for life. For some the warnings did not take hold.

We were an excited bunch of "swabbies" getting ready for our first liberty. We spit-shined our black shoes to a high gloss, put on our dress uniforms, and squared our white hats just so. We took the bus into downtown San Diego and joined the sea of other white hats filling the streets.

I spent an enjoyable day visiting Balboa Park and the San Diego Zoo and kept out of trouble. That wasn't true for some of the guys. More than a few came back to the base red-faced with drink, proudly showing tattooed arms covered with eagles, anchors, and snarling panthers.

Finally, graduation day. Our company, along with a number of others, filed onto the parade ground and marched in review past Navy brass to the thrilling strains of "Anchors Away." I was proud to be a sailor.

It was December 8, 1952, and boot camp was finally over. I was given leave and spent Christmas with my family in Montgomery. My orders were then to report to the Navy's Airman "Class P" School in Norman, Oklahoma. It would be an eight-week course at a preparatory level for the broad field of naval aviation.

It was a cold day during the first week in January, 1953, when I reported in to the training center, a collection of barracks and administrative buildings, on the dusty wind-swept prairie near Norman, about 15 miles south of Oklahoma City. I hoisted the sea bag on my shoulder and went to barracks 63 and found a bunk.

It felt like I had walked in on a funeral. There was a small group of southern boys almost in tears as they sat around a small radio listening to the records of a country western singer. I asked around and was told Hank Williams had died. (Hank Williams, Sr. died in his sleep in the back seat of his Cadillac on Jan. 1, 1953, at the age of 29.) It didn't mean much to me. I knew little about Hank Williams, having grown up hearing German and Czech polkas and Russ Morgan and his big band.

The course work at the school wasn't very exciting—primarily basic mathematics and physics—and the instructors seemed bored teaching it. The first class I had in the morning was physics, and the instructor was a second-class petty officer in his 20s with a red nose and paunch. He was a drinker and would come into class hung over, his hand quivering as he chain-smoked cigarettes and drank mug after mug of black coffee.

I had been at the school in Norman about a month when my mother and Grandma Holey came to visit me. They took the Rock Island train and stayed at the Black Hotel in Oklahoma City for about three days. I went window-shopping with them, and Mom and I went to the movies. I felt sorry I didn't have a car to take them around, but they said they had had a good time.

The jobs in the Navy were called "ratings," and they were grouped according to related knowledge and skills. The Aviation Group had about 13 ratings, including such jobs as air control man, aviation electrician's mate, aviation machinist's mate, etc. The sailors at Norman's P School would be placed into one of the 13 ratings based on their grades, aptitude, and preference. Then, after graduation, they would be sent to an "A" School for intensive training in that particular rating.

I narrowed my preference in ratings to first aerographer's mate, and if not that then photographer's mate or aviation storekeeper. The A Schools for these ratings were scattered across the country. The school for aerographer's mate was in Lakehurst, New Jersey.

Just before graduation, I was told I would be going to Aerographer's (Class A) School. I had done well at Norman, graduating 35th out of a class of 611.

There was a damp chill in the air that second week in March 1953, when I arrived at the U.S. Naval Air Station at Lakehurst,

N.J., about 10 miles from the Atlantic Ocean. NAS Lakehurst was the headquarters for the Navy's Lighter-Than-Air program. I marveled at the huge hangars on the base for housing the Navy's massive helium-filled airships. These blimps had been developed during the 1930s and used in World War II for patrolling, hunting submarines, and escorting convoys. I remembered that here at Lakehurst occurred a terrible disaster in 1937 when Germany's giant Zeppelin, the "Hindenburg" burst into flames just before landing, killing 35 of 97 persons aboard. And it was here I'd be spending the next 15 weeks studying aerology.

I was one of 56 Navy airman apprentices and marines that mustered for our first class roll call at the Aerographer's A School. We were welcomed by two petty officers. The first, an aerographer's mate first class (AG1) was our lead instructor and had a strange facial tick. He would clench his teeth in a way that made his cheek muscles knot and his neck swell. He got right to the point.

"Boys," the AG1 said, "I'll warn you right now. You'd better knuckle down and study, because your grades will decide where you go after you graduate from here. You see, the number one guy in class gets first pick of duty stations available—and down the line to the last guy who gets what's left. We have weather stations scattered on islands all over the Pacific; some places it's just you and the gooney birds."

So it was with this admonition in the back of our minds that we began an intense study of weather and weather forecasting. We learned about air masses, those huge bodies of warm or cold air that constantly move across the earth's surface, and the development of fronts (cold, warm, stationary, and occluded) that form when air masses of contrasting temperatures converge.

We learned that clouds herald the approach of a front, from the high, wispy cirrus clouds that develop as a warm front draws near, often bringing a slow, steady rain or snow, to the dark, ominous cumulonimbus clouds that tower quickly to altitudes as high as 70,000 feet in advance of a swiftly-moving cold front, often resulting in high winds, lightning, and sometimes large hail and even tornadoes.

We learned about the formation of high and low air pressure systems, and the relationship of a rapidly "falling barometer" with the approach of a violent tropical cyclone—and the calamity that can occur when that weather indicator is not sufficiently regarded.

We studied the six elements that are used to describe weather: wind, air pressure, air temperature, humidity, clouds, and precipitation—and we studied the instruments to measure them: anemometer, barometer, thermometer, rain gauge, etc.

We were told how important it was to be accurate in our weather observations and calculations, as the lives of our shipmates depended on it. The message got through to me. In a letter to my mother I expressed concern about making mistakes.

Lakehurst was not all study, though. On weekends, if I did not have the duty, I tried to get out and see the sights. New Jersey is noted for its beautiful seashore along the Atlantic Ocean. I went to Asbury Park, a well-known resort town along the Jersey Shore, and walked along the boardwalk and ate saltwater taffy.

New York City wasn't far away, and it drew me like iron to a magnet. In a letter to Mom I reported one experience in the Big Apple:

Last week I went to New York City with my roommate. We went to the Museum of Natural History, Empire State Building, a YMCA dance, and saw Eddie Fisher in person at the Paramount Theater. We also saw the new type of movie they have now—three-dimensional. We had to have special polarized glasses to see it, but it certainly was a thrill. Everything seemed as if you were actually there. In one scene, two men were fighting and one threw a chair at the other. That chair seemed as if it was coming right at me.

I remember being on Times Square at midnight one Saturday night with a buddy. I couldn't believe all the people and bright lights. And we went to Coney Island and rode the rollercoaster. We met some girls. They though we were from "down South" because of our accent.

Finally, June 16, 1953—graduation day. Now we could find out where each of us would spend the next two years of our naval career. We were called into a room. Our instructors had listed on a chalkboard all the available duty stations with job openings (billets) for Aerographer's Mates. Opposite the duty stations were listed the 56 graduates, starting with the best student on top, then down to the guy with the worst grades at the bottom.

The AG1, the instructor with the tick, called out the top man and asked his choice. The top guy, a quiet and serious sort, looked over the list. He had plenty of options. There were weather stations with vacancies all over the world: Alaska, Port-Lyautey in Morocco, Guantanamo Bay in Cuba, the Panama Canal Zone, naval air stations all over the U.S. and Hawaii, as well as U.S. ships (mostly the big ones, aircraft carriers and battleships). To our surprise, he took a billet on a stateside naval air station: NAS Corpus Christi in Texas.

Several of us in the middle of the class standing (I was 19th) were holding our breath. "Frenchy," one of our instructors, was a colorful character and advised us on the good and bad billets on the list. During World War II he had been a weather observer on an island off the coast of New Guinea. He said the girls there took a while to get used to, but after a few years he didn't want to leave. He said the best duty on the list was at the fleet weather central in Japan; it had five openings.

John Lund, 18th in the class, and I wanted Japan. We watched in dismay as the 17th man took the 5th and last slot. The next best, we thought, was the fleet weather central in the Philippine Islands where there were two billets. John took the first and I the second.

John and I were excited. We were going to the Philippine Islands—the "Pearl of the Orient." Our orders were to report to the naval base on Treasure Island in San Francisco Bay in California. There we would catch a ship to take us to the P. I.

We boarded a train and headed west. When we arrived, we were assigned to the transient barracks and told we might have to wait a few weeks before a transport ship going to the P. I. would be available.

While we waited there wasn't much to do. First thing in the morning we'd muster at the masters-at-arms (MAA) office for assignment; usually some clean-up job—then we were free to go on liberty.

I took every opportunity to take liberty in San Francisco. It was so convenient. The S.F.-Oakland Bay Bridge went right across Treasure Island. City buses stopped at the gate of the naval station and went downtown. There was so much to see: the hills, the views, the bays and bridges. And it was in San Francisco where I learned about homosexuality—first hand.

It was a sunny late afternoon and I was in a cable car exploring San Francisco for the first time. I was in uniform: those natty form-fitting dress blues. The trousers were the old style, with the flap over the crotch and secured by thirteen buttons, rather than a zipper.

At one stop, a portly middle-aged man in a business suit got on. He sidled up to me and started talking. He seemed friendly. He asked me if I was new in San Francisco, and when I said yes, offered to show me the town. He was an attorney, he said, on his way home. We could stop at his place for a drink or two, then go out for dinner—his treat. I was accustomed to "Minnesota nice" people and in my naïveté said sure, why not?

The man took me to an exclusive residential district. The building we entered was of stone enclosed by a high wrought iron fence. The name of the building, the ... Arms, was embossed on a shield at the entrance.

The man's apartment was large with conservative furnishings. He motioned me to a sofa to sit and said he'd mix drinks. As soon as I sat down, however, he was at my side. His demeanor changed; he was excited. He tried to put his arm around me and with the other had, fumbled with the buttons at my waist. I was taken aback for a moment, unable to respond. I grabbed his hand and pushed it away and got up. I started to leave and he clung to my arm, pleading for me to stay. He took my hand in his, caressing my palm with his fingers. I jerked my hand free and hurried out the door—shaken, my emotions in turmoil.

At this time of my life I knew little about homosexuality. If I thought about it at all, it was something perverse. I knew it was definitely a "no-no" in the Navy, however.

Finally, I got my orders and boarded one of the Navy's MSTS (Military Sea Transportation Service) ships. It would take three weeks to get to the Philippine Islands with stops in Hawaii and Guam on the way. We weighed anchor and slowly sailed under the Golden Gate Bridge. The deck was lined with men, their faces all turned eastward as we watched the Golden Gate fade from view.

Our living quarters aboard ship were cramped and not geared for comfort. The bunks were racks of four or five tightly strung canvas hammocks stacked one on top of the other—each about a foot and a half apart. Your face was just inches below the man above you.

Since we were not part of the ship's crew, we had little to do. So we spent the daylight hours playing cards, writing letters, watching flying fish, or reading paperbacks. I can still see myself—above decks one sunny afternoon sitting in the shade, my back against a bulkhead and the ocean breeze cooling my face, reading an absorbing story about a western gunfighter in the book *Shane.*

A few days out from San Francisco we hit rough water. For most of us it caused no problem. But a few got terribly seasick. I remember one unpleasant event. Four guys were playing cards topside. All of a sudden a seasick man from below decks came storming up and rushed to the side of the ship. He threw up over the railing. A strong wind was blowing inboard, however. It sprayed vomit back and splattered the faces of the card players. There was a howl of anger. For a moment I thought they were going to throw the seasick fellow overboard. Naturally, those of us left unscathed roared with laughter.

We arrived in Honolulu for a brief stopover and were allowed to leave the ship for an afternoon of sightseeing. Several of us took a tour. We saw the Royal Hawaiian Hotel on Waikiki and stopped at the Blow-Hole to watch the water spew in the air. We went to the National Memorial Cemetery of the Pacific in the Punchbowl Crater and saw the grave of Ernie Pyle, the war correspondent killed by Japanese machine-gun bullets in World War II. We toured the Dole pineapple factory. I was amazed when I went to take a drink at a water fountain and pineapple juice came out instead of water.

While still in the Hawaiian Islands, we got great news. On July 27, 1953, the Korean War ended with the signing of an armistice at Panmunjom. We didn't have that to worry about anymore.

We left Honolulu, crossed the International Date Line, and steamed into the big U.S. naval base on Guam—a rugged, tropical island about two thirds of the way between Hawaii and Manila. We were not allowed to leave the ship. After a brief stay, unloading cargo and taking on a few passengers, we left for the Philippine Islands.

The Philippine Islands

SEVERAL DAYS LATER we entered the South China Sea. Soon we saw land. It was Luzon, the largest and northernmost island in the Philippine Archipelago, a chain of 7,083 islands stretching over 1,166 miles.

We sailed into Manila Bay. About 40 miles long, it was here in 1898 that Commodore George Dewey defeated the Spanish naval force during the Spanish-American War and wrested control of the islands from Spain. The Philippine Islands became a U.S. colony. Guarding the inlet to the bay was Corregidor, the small rocky island that was the last bastion of Filipino and American forces fighting the Japanese during World War II.

Someone pointed out Sangley Point, a slender thumb-like strip jutting out into Manila Bay. At the time of the War, it was the site of the Cavite Navy Yard, home of the U.S. Asiatic Fleet and a major ship repair facility. On December 10, 1941, several days after Pearl Harbor, Japanese planes bombed and battered Cavite. Ships were destroyed and sailors killed in the base area. Remains of the sunken ships could still be seen. In some cases a large part of a ship was above water. We were told Filipino fishermen and their families lived on some of these rusted hulks. Now the area was Sangley Point Naval Air station, my home for the next two years.

It was the height of the rainy season when I reported in to the Fleet Weather Central. Monsoon winds were driving the rain in sheets, rattling against the corrugated metal roof of the double-sized Quonset hut. Chief Petty Officer Kenneth "Shady" Lane welcomed me aboard. During a brief lull in the rain, a fellow on section watch helped load my gear into a jeep. We drove a few blocks through standing water to a line of Quonset huts at the end of the base.

"This is home," the sailor said, pulling in front of a hut with a banana tree in front. "Two guys rotated back to the states a few days ago so there are a couple of empty bunks."

I grabbed my sea bag and splashed through ankle-deep water to the door. I walked into a darkened room, canvas roll-ups pulled down over the screens. A light bulb illuminated a table with four card players. There was a smell of dampness and mold. A radio tuned to the Armed Force radio station was playing "Swanee River Boogie" by Glen Gray and the Casa Loma Orchestra.

After introduction and handshakes all around, I dumped my sodden sea bag on an empty bed on one of the 20 or so double metal bunks in the hut. I started sorting out dirty clothes and asked about a laundry. One of the card players said not to worry. "You're in the P.I. now," he said. "We have a Filipino hut boy that'll take your dirty clothes to the laundry, shine your shoes, and make your bed. All you have to do is put on clean clothes and take off the dirty ones. He does the rest. We each kick in a little each month to pay him." It turned out that Filipino civilians did just about all the menial tasks on the base.

Later, I joined a few of the boys and ran through the rain to the mess hall for the evening meal. On the way, one of the guys said Manila was just across the bay, about eight miles—easy to see on a clear day. Two weeks later, when it stopped raining, I saw the capital city of the Philippine Islands for the first time.

After chow we went to the Enlisted Men's Club for drinks. Jim, an AG2 and one of the Fleet Weather Central section leaders, filled me in. "The best way to save money in the P.I.," Jim laughed, "is to be an alcoholic. You can get drunk every night for less than a buck." In a way, he was right. Drinks were cheap at the EM Club. Beer was 10 cents, mixed drinks 15 cents, and you could buy a bottle of Canadian Club whiskey for $1.25. I ordered a Pabst Blue Ribbon beer.

"Jesus," Jim said, "don't drink that horse piss." He called to the bartender, "Make that a San Miguel for the man." He nodded to me. "He just came in from the states. He don't know any better."

San Miguel Pale Pilson. I had a few that night and felt it. It was good beer, but strong. "Over 6 percent," Jim said. "It's brewed in Manila. Some say that General MacArthur owned part of the San Miguel Brewing Company before the war."

My first watch at Sangley Point Fleet Weather Central was a day watch starting at 0800 hours in the morning. Carroll, my section leader, a serious, soft-spoken AG1, took me into a small conference room. On the wall was a map of the Pacific Ocean. "There are three Navy Fleet Weather Centrals responsible for weather forecasting in this area," he said. "One there," he pointed to Japan, "another in the Hawaiian Islands, and a third here at Sangley. Our responsibility covers this section," he swept his hand in a wide arc around the Philippine Islands that extended north to Formosa, east to Guam, south to the equator, and west across the South China Sea. "We issue weather forecasts and storm warnings to ships at sea and naval stations—around the clock, 24 hours a day."

One of the section crew I'd seen plotting a weather map came in and announced there was fresh coffee. We filled mugs. I lit a cigarette. Carroll went on. "Typhoons, though are our big concern here," he said. "A typhoon can be a killer if it hits our ships or a naval base. Our job is to locate and track them and warn the fleet."

It didn't take long for me to learn a good deal about typhoons (called hurricanes in North America). We were in the middle of typhoon season, June to October, and could expect up to 20 each year in our area of responsibility. They usually started out near the equator. Hot, moist air was sucked up from the ocean, creating a whirling cyclone with furious winds and torrential rain. Covering an area from 100 to 600 miles wide and traveling between five and twelve miles per hour, a typhoon tended to move northwest along or across the Philippine Islands, often doing great damage to buildings, bridges, and crops—then sweeping across the South China Sea to hit Vietnam, or swerving further north to strike Formosa or Japan.

During World War II the Navy learned the destructive force of a typhoon through an appalling naval disaster. In December 1944, Admiral William "Bull" Halsey's Third Fleet was near the Philippine Islands. The fleet, in support of General MacArthur's invasion of the islands, was sending carrier planes to attack and bomb Japanese strongholds. On December 18th, a powerful typhoon hammered the fleet, causing grave damage to many ships and planes. Three destroyers were capsized and sunk, taking 790 sailors down to a watery grave.

Survivors of the typhoon reported terrifying experiences. Winds of up to 120 knots screeched and howled through the ships' riggings and guy wires. The spray and spume ripped at the faces of lookouts and signalmen, drawing blood from cheeks and foreheads. One destroyer was completely lost from view as it slid into the trough of a 60-foot wave.

Sailors fighting the storm's fury were swept overboard, never to be seen again. To save his men, the captain of one aircraft carrier instituted a two-man deck order: no seaman was allowed topside unless roped to a shipmate.

One of the few survivors of a lost destroyer gave this heart-breaking account. As the heaving sea hammered the ship, down in the hold he heard some men praying and others singing The Navy Hymn: "Eternal father, strong to save, Whose arm hath bound the restless wave...Oh, hear us when we cry to Thee, For those in peril on the sea..." just as the destroyed rolled over and went to the bottom.

The Navy held a Court of Inquiry. The findings included criticism of the failure of fleet's weather forecasting staff to correctly locate and plot the path of the typhoon. As a result, the Third Fleet had run right into the middle of the typhoon. Some said the fleet's aerology officer was hampered by a dearth of weather information on which to locate the typhoon. Others thought he relied too heavily on guidance from the Fleet Weather Central in Hawaii, some 4,000 miles away.

Whatever the true fact, the Navy took action to prevent another such tragedy. After the war, Fleet Weather Centrals were established at naval bases in Japan and the Philippine Islands. More weather reporting stations were set up.

The FWC had a total complement of about 60 officers and men; about two thirds of whom were divided into five sections. Each section worked three eight-hour shifts in a 72-hour period: a day watch (0800 to 1600), an evening watch (1600 to 2400) and a mid-watch (2400-0800). Then we had three days off. We could walk out the gate on liberty at eight in the morning after mid-watch and not come back until the start of our day watch 72 hours later. Fantastic duty.

Each section had about six men to gather, plot, and transmit weather information and forecasts. The flow of work started with one man who took observations. Every hour he would walk up a ladder to the top of our building where the instruments were located. There, he would observe and record the temperature, air pressure, wind direction and velocity, cloud cover, and precipitation.

This information was coded and typed on a teletypewriter as perforations on tape. At a precise time each hour the tape was taken to an automatic transmitter and the weather report sent out.

As this was happening, another section hand was manning two rows of Teletype receivers, ripping off sheets of coded weather observations coming in from weather stations on land and sea. He dropped the sheets into a box next to a man at a drawing table. This fellow had a weather map covered with tiny circles. Each circle was the location of a reporting station. As the reports came in, he decoded and plotted the information on and around the reporting station's circle.

When plotted, the weather map was taken to the duty officer. He analyzed it and wrote up a forecast. Another section staffer typed it up and drove it a few blocks to the base communications center for transmission to navy land installations and ships at sea.

We monitored upper air conditions using weather balloons. This was a two-man job. John, an old-timer in my section, checked me out. He took me into a back room filled with helium tanks and boxes of pilot balloons (Pibals). He attached a balloon to a helium tank and blew it up. "Watch this," John said, and went through a familiar routine he pulled on every new guy. He inhaled helium and started talking. His voice sounded weird and strangled, high-pitched and funny. He told a joke and laughed.

We took the balloon out on the landing strip. I held it while John set up a surveyor's telescope called a theodolite. On his signal, I released the balloon and he tracked it through the theodolite. By determining the balloon's direction and angle above the horizon, we could calculate wind speed and direction at various altitudes.

Along with Pibals, we sent up radiosondes: balloons with a radio transmitter attached that recorded the pressure, temperature, and relative humidity as it ascended. This information was transmitted to a ground receiver. We tracked the radiosonde with the theodolite until it was out of sight. The balloon might climb 15 miles or more in the air before it burst, dropping the instrument package to earth (usually in the ocean) beneath a tiny parachute.

A tough job was trying to track a weather balloon in gale-force winds. I remember desperately trying to locate a balloon, just released, in the theodolite—then struggling to keep it in sight—almost impossible.

A few months after I arrived, Robert (Bob) Vaughn came aboard FWC. Several years older than me, Bob had previously served in the Army or Air Force and transferred in as an AG Petty Officer—soon to become my Section Leader. A gentle guy, with a soft Kentucky way of talking, Bob had a fun sense of humor and soon became my best friend. A lover of poetry, he kidded me and called me "Blackie," after California's legendary stagecoach robber of the 1870s, Black Bart, who scrawled poems and left them at the scenes of his robberies, one of which read:

I've labored long and hard for bread
For honor and for riches
But on my corns too long you've tread
You fine-haired sons of Bitches

BLACK BART, the Poet

In the months that followed, Bob Vaughn and I and several other shipmates took leave and went sight seeing. We went to Hong Kong on the east coast of China, and spent a couple of days shopping for clothes and eating at fancy restaurants.

My shipmates and I browsed the many curio stores. The Chinese shopkeepers expected us to bargain, so we did. When they said something was ten dollars, we said we'd pay six. We would usually get the item for seven or eight dollars.

I purchased a Chinese chest of teakwood covered with carvings of old Chinese wise men, trees, and birds. I paid 45 dollars American for it and filled the chest with other purchases I planned to take back to the states: Irish linen for Mom and Chinese carvings for Dad and my brother Milt.

We toured Manila, the Islands' capital city; Baguio, the summer capital in the mountains of Luzon; and Corregidor, the old island fortress at the mouth of Manila Bay.

By the end of 1954, I had spent about 15 months at the FWC. I had been promoted to Aerographer's Mate Third Class and was getting bored with weather maps and Teletype machines. An opportunity arose to spend six months temporary duty on the base Armed Forces Police.

The base Armed Forces Police was responsible for maintaining order among military personnel in Cavite. It was commanded by a captain in the Marine Corps. Volunteers from each of the divisions on the base filled out the detachment. The volunteer from the Fleet Weather Central was completing his tour and someone had to fill his spot. I signed up and got the job.

The Sangley AFP was housed in a Quonset hut on the main drag of the base. It had a small office facing the street with a counter, two desks, and file cabinets and quarters for the enlisted men (two-tiered bunks and lockers) in the back. I moved my gear from the FWC hut and took a top bunk with my new shipmates—the police patrol.

On my first day on the job I was issued a white helmet with the block letters AFP on the front, a web belt, and a wooden baton. A veteran of the AFP checked me out on Cavite City, our area of responsibility. He said there were about 50 bars and clubs within the town to provide entertainment for sailors on liberty. And, he continued, wherever there were bars, booze, and girls, there could be trouble. It was our job to keep it under control.

The AFP, like police in the states, operated on the buddy system. My first partner was a "volunteer," not his choice, from the Coast

Guard, earnest and taciturn, finishing the last month of his six-month tour and anxious to get back to his job as coxswain of a coastal boat. We were a foot patrol, walking an eight-block beat from the base's main gate to the center of Cavite City.

Our job, walking the beat, was to check the bars, stopping in to "show the flag," letting the white hats and bar men know we were on duty. If we smelled trouble—a sailor arguing over his bar bill or squabbling with a bar girl, or sailors from different ships trying to out-macho one another—we intervened to stop the dispute before it got out of hand.

About every block we walked was a club or bar catering to American sailors. For most, there was a tired similarity. Each had a jukebox filled with popular stateside songs, a bar, a few tables and chairs, room enough for handful of dancers, and three or more bar girls.

Here and there would be little neighborhood open-air stores— one like another. You'd see a lean-to with a corrugated iron roof, and Coca Cola or 7Up signs nailed to its support poles. A counter would run along the front and sides, lined with covered glass jars of candy, cookies, bread rolls, and anything else that needed protection from flies and the humidity. There'd be baskets of fruits and vegetables, and bunches of bananas hanging from a rope across the ceiling. A group of young boys might be grab-assing on a bench out front, and a mongrel dog tiptoeing around puddles of water still standing from the rains. And maybe an old woman in a large peaked palm-leaf hat would be sitting on her haunches nearby with baskets of fresh-caught fish for sale.

Since we were in the same bars often, we got to know some of the bar girls. One of them, "Rosie," was older and whenever we came into the bar she would call me "Chinese eyes," because of my Clint Eastwood squint. It wasn't an affectation on my part. I wasn't wearing glasses, and it was two years later at Sand Point

Naval Air Station in Seattle when I learned I was nearsighted as well as astigmatic. (I was fitted with glasses after an eye exam when I complained my eyes hurt when plotting weather maps.)

Rosie had a stream of chat geared to keep a sailor glued to her table and buying drinks until his money ran out. It involved a good deal of sex talk.

Rosie had been a teenager during the Japanese occupation of the Philippine Islands in World War II. She asked me if I knew the difference between Japanese soldiers and American sailors. I got a kick out of this talk and played along. "No, what?"

"I'll show you," Rosie said. With one hand she made a circle using her index finger and thumb. With the other hand she pulled a tuft of her skirt through the circle to form the shape of a penis about four inches long. "That Japanese soldier," she said. Then she pulled the dress further out to about seven inches and waggled it. "That American sailor!" She reached over, poked my shoulder and laughed.

When my six-month tour with the AFP was over I transferred back to the FWC. In May 1955, I was promoted to Aerographer's Mate Second Class (AG2). My two-year stint in the Philippine Islands would be over in August 1955.

While I was waiting for my orders, a remarkable celestial phenomenon occurred: a total solar eclipse. As meteorologists, we knew it was coming and were excited.

The eclipse completely hid the sun at 12:20 on June 21, 1955. That day the sky was clear and the sun shown bright, and then it became dark as night. We could see two stars. It was eerie. When it was completely dark, quite a few natives, who didn't know it was going to happen, were a little shook up. The eclipse lasted about seven minutes. Chickens must have gone to roost in the dark. When the sun emerged, the roosters started crowing.

As my tour of duty was coming to an end, I thought about the weather we had seen in the Philippine Islands. Typhoons were the one weather phenomenon we feared most. Although some had struck in FWC's area of responsibility, the vast southeast Pacific, none had hit Sangley Point; we had been spared their lash.

Finally, my orders came in. I left by ship in August, took leave, and traveled by train to Minnesota. When I got home I went right to work. But Montgomery didn't feel like home and neither did the meat market. Well, I thought, I will just have to keep at it.

When my leave was up, I drove to my new duty station: Sand Point Naval Air Station in Seattle, Washington. Dad had gotten a new 1955 Mercury and gave me his 1951 Chevrolet. Mom wanted to come with me, stay a few weeks in Seattle, and come back home by train.

I was in uniform when Mom and I struck out across Montana and Idaho to Seattle. Mom was an attractive woman and at 44 years of age looked 10 years younger. When we stopped at small-town cafés along the way, we often drew curious glances—and sometimes stares. I guess a young sailor with an older woman with no evidence of a wedding ring on my hand just didn't look right.

We got to Seattle and Mom checked into a downtown hotel. We spent several days sightseeing before Mom left for Minnesota. The naval station was on Sand Point, a peninsula in North Seattle that juts into Lake Washington. For years it had served as an air base, aviation training center, and aircraft repair depot for the U.S. Navy. After the end of the Korean War, its role was reduced and when I arrived its primary function was as a naval reserve training base.

I drove to the base and the Fleet Weather Central. I gave my orders to the first class yeoman handling personnel and wandered over to introduce myself to the heavy-set section leader leaning over a plotting map.

"It rains a lot but you won't have to worry about typhoons," he grinned, shaking my hand. He poured me a cup of coffee and walked me up to the observation deck. It was a sunny day and the section leader pointed to the southeast and a stunning snow-capped mountain. "That is Mount Rainier. It's 60 miles away, and you don't often see it, rainy and cloudy as it is so often here."

The section leader showed me around the FWC, smaller than at Sangley Point, and at lunchtime took me to the mess hall. I spent the rest of the afternoon getting checked out and at the end of the day watch, followed two of my new shipmates to our "digs," a two-story barracks. Our outfit was lodged on the second floor.

In May of 1956, I got promoted to first class aerographer's mate and to section leader as well. And on top of that, I was made barracks supervisor over 40 white hats. I was accountable for more than myself now. With four months to go before my discharge, I found that I was pretty good as a supervisor. I treated the men as I would have wanted to be treated—the "golden rule." I had no discipline problems.

With the section running smooth and the weather mild with few surprises, work was easy. The hours dragged, especially the mid-watches, midnight to 0800 hours. To pass the time, I read books from the base library. One project was to read the complete volume of Sherlock Holmes short stories. I read most of them. Another diversion was music. The radio dial in the office was set for a constant rendition of the current Top 40 songs. There was always someone mouthing the lyrics or whistling softly the current hot number. My taste centered on the sentimental ballads by songsters like Frank Sinatra, Tony Bennett, and Jo Stafford, and the vocal groups: the Ames Brothers and the Four Aces. The first time we heard Elvis Presley sing "Hound Dog," one guy said, "What the hell kind of music is that?" reflecting our general thinking. Rock n' roll was foreign to us, not at all romantic.

A few weeks before my discharge, our skipper, Commander Paul T. Jorgensen, called me into his office. He had my service record in his hand. "You've done good work here, and you have a clean record. We would like you to reenlist, make the Navy a career." I thanked him, then told him of my promise to my parents to go back to the meat market to help out. He nodded in understanding, shook my hand, and offered me "good luck."

On September 7, 1956, I took my mustering-out pay of $300, a Good Conduct Medal, and walked out of the Fleet Weather Central office a free man. Two of my shipmates got their discharges the same day. Their homes were on the East Coast. Since I was the only one with a car, I asked them to join me, and we would share driving on a round-the-clock jaunt to Minneapolis. From there, they could take a bus or train east.

Official U.S. Navy photograph, Barton Conrad Bauer, served 1952 to 1956

Holding onto a bunch of bananas outside my living quarters on Sangley
Point in P.I., 1953.

Plotting weather maps
at Sangley Point Naval
Air Station, P.I. Fleet
Weather Central, 1954

Christmas card, 1954

Volunteered and served on U.S. Armed Forces
Police in Cavite City in P.I. Six months temporary
duty.

23.

Home and Conflict

THE DAY AFTER I got home, I was back in the shop behind the counter working. Lindy Linberger, welcomed me and offered to help in any way. My job was to work with Lindy and learn as much as I could. Dad said little about the future. I assumed he wanted me to handle Lindy's job some day. Lindy never said anything to me, but looking back he must have worried a little about his job security.

As time went on, my interest in the work waned; I went through the motions, but my heart wasn't in it. And to complicate matters, I started dating a waitress at the café across the street from our meat market. Within weeks we started going steady—going out just about every other night. My father must have noticed, but said nothing. Seeing me drag around the shop with "no fire in the belly" must have grated. Dad was a high-energy guy, enthusiastic, and hard working. I can just imagine him thinking, "That slacker can't be my son."

Then it came. About three months after I came home, Dad exploded and called me a liar. It was a minor thing: a misunderstanding on a small meat delivery to a local restaurant, the details of which I can't remember. I protested that the mistake in the order was not mine, but the restaurant owner's. For whatever reason, our argument escalated, became heated, and finally in response to my justification, Dad whispered through clenched teeth, "That's a lie," then turned and walked away.

I was stunned. To argue and then be called a liar by my father. This had never happened before. I could never remember even quarreling with him. Granted, I was always the docile, subservient first son, never questioning his orders. But now something was different.

Perhaps it was me. After four years in the Navy, advancing to section petty officer in a fleet weather central and a barracks petty officer over 40 men, I had changed. At 24 years of age, I had been stationed from one end of the United States to the other, had spent two years in the Philippine Islands, and was no longer the compliant son I had been.

But there was more. I began to realize I'd made a big mistake in coming back to the meat market. I no longer wanted to be a butcher, stuck in this small provincial town in southern Minnesota, hands bloody from slaughtering animals and cutting meat. I wanted something better. But how would I get out of this predicament—and then what would I do?

When I went into the Navy I had promised my father and mother I would come back and work with Dad in the shop. During the four years away, I reassured them in my letters home I could not wait to get back. I took Navy correspondence courses on small business operation to better prepare myself. My parents were counting on me to step in and help carry the burden of running the business.

And to make things more difficult, my younger brother, Milt, my only sibling, had decided to forgo the family operation and had enrolled as a freshman at Macalester College with thoughts of a profession like veterinary medicine. I'm sure he felt comfortable doing so since I would be the one to carry on the Bauer tradition as our father had done when his father retired.

In the days that followed, the quarrel with my father was never discussed. No apologies were made by either side. As usual, mother said little—completely submissive to Dad, the tension simmering just below the surface.

What to do? Father was not one to discuss feelings—his or mine—or plans for the future. Growing up, I shared problems, hopes and dreams with Mom, never with Dad. He was accustomed to working hard six days a week, from dawn to dusk. Even Sundays involved work: feeding cattle on the farm, or making hay if the weather was right, or butchering for the meat market. Until the last few years when he and Mom started to travel, my father's chief pastime was hunting, and coon hunting was done primarily at night in the autumn months.

Finally, I decided. I could not continue living at home and working in the meat market, taking orders from my father until he died or grew too feeble to run the business as had happened with my grandfather. But what were my alternatives?

I looked into employment in weather forecasting; however, little was available. There were only two positions open, both as a meteorologist with the federal government. One was at Flying Cloud airport near Shakopee, Minnesota. The other was near a remote Eskimo village: Point Barrow—the northernmost spot in Alaska on the Arctic Ocean. As an inducement the latter job required only six months of the year on Point Barrow, the other six months in Seattle, Washington. Both jobs were paying $300 per month, not bad in 1956.

However, as much as I enjoyed my career as an Aerographer's Mate in the Navy, it was the exotic places and fun times that I remembered fondly, not the work. Gathering and analyzing weather data, drawing up weather maps, and predicting weather was not my strong suit. If I had to grade my technical skills in these areas, it would be a C-plus or a B-minus at best. Also, to advance in weather forecasting as a civilian would require a college degree, preferably in meteorology—coursework in which I had little interest.

The other fork in the road could be college. Before enlisting in the U.S. Navy, I had completed three semesters at Wartburg and one semester at Macalester. My grades were good, so I could return or transfer to another school. With four years and an honorable discharge from the Navy, I was eligible for the G.I. Bill.

I started leaning toward college. I wondered about the field of study I would follow. Looking back, I have a vivid image of sitting on the edge of my bed, running my finger through a University of Minnesota catalog index of courses—starting with Astronomy down to Zoology.

In 24 years, I had been exposed to a fairly wide variety of academic and vocational experiences. I learned what I liked and what turned me off, what I could do and what was a struggle. Algebra, physics, statistics, and foreign languages were tough and uninteresting. History, literature, psychology, sociology, and political science came easy, and were absorbing. My strength was working with and through people, not things. Building houses, fixing cars, or manipulating the numbers on a balance sheet was not for me—but people were endlessly fascinating. I wanted to know what made them tick, why they did what they did and, in a sense, by knowing people better—get a better handle on my own psyche. So the direction of my study was clear.

Leaving for college, however, involved yet another complication. It was an "affair of the heart." In September, about two weeks after my discharge, I started dating a woman whom I had become very fond of. She was a waitress in a restaurant across the street from Bauer's Meat Market where we delivered meat. Blond, buxom, and curvaceous, with a flirtatious eye, she captured my fancy from the first time I saw her—a scene as clear today as if looking at a home movie.

It was 1955. I was home in Montgomery on a 30-day leave from Sand Point Naval Air Station in Seattle helping my father in the meat market: me in the front behind the meat counter and my father in the back room cutting meat. There was a temporary lull in mid-afternoon with no customers in the shop. Suddenly the door flew open and in bounced this saucy little blond in her sexy white waitress uniform. With hardly a glance in my direction, she headed straight to the back room. I could hear her laughing and kidding my father: something about the steak he delivered being too tough. Although in his fifties and somewhat reserved by nature, my father flushed with pleasure at the attention of this pretty 20-year-old woman. Within minutes she was out the door and gone—leaving me wondering who she was and from whence she had come. In a small town you knew everyone, but I had been away too long. Father said her name was Shirley, that she had been raised on a farm near LeCenter, and that she had been a waitress at the café for about four or five years. He said that the previous owners of the café told him Shirley was "the best waitress they ever had."

Now after three months of "going steady," I found myself caring for "Shirl" a great deal. Leaving town for college could not be allowed to jeopardize this relationship.

In the end, I enrolled at Macalester College on the G.I. Bill. Several months later Shirley joined me; we got an apartment in St. Paul, and were married in April 1957. Eventually, I transferred to the University of Minnesota and got a B.A. degree, and later in 1961 a Master's Degree in Social Work. Thirty years later, after stints as a caseworker, a hospital social worker, and 20 plus years as a supervisor with the Minnesota Department of Welfare/Human Services in St. Paul, I retired in June 1990.

with Lindy in our meat market in Montgomery, 1956

First picture of Shirl and I together at my parents' home, Nov. 1956. A
gorgeous woman, lucky me!

Left: Shirley, about 5 years old

Below: Barton Bauer and Shirley Pendergast were married on April 13, 1957 at Reformation Lutheran Church, on Oxford and Laurel in St. Paul.

A family gathering at Aunt Esther and Dorothy Bauer's house in St. Paul about 1971. Dad is at the head of the table with Shirley and I on his left, then our son Brent, Lena Lehman, a cousin, in pink, son Jeff, Dorothy and Esther standing, son Scott, Mom, Milt's wife Betty, and their son Steve. The empty chair at Dad's right was probably my brother Milt's who was taking the picture.

Shirl and I on our 50th wedding anniversary in 2007 with our sons and their families (grandchildren and great grandchildren)

VI. DEATH *and the* HEREAFTER

24.

Death—Still a Mystery

IT IS NOW 2012, 18 years after my father's death. I am even more stooped over—5'6". My heartbeat is not regular and I get breathless walking up a flight of stairs.

Although my body is frail, my mind is still good. But my time is growing short. Death intrudes on my thoughts more often now. Nightmares come when I least expect them, reminding me of what lies ahead.

Several weeks ago, about three in the morning, I was shocked awake from a deep sleep, my eyes wide with fear, my heart pounding. I had dreamt I was in a cemetery standing near an open grave. There were two gravediggers, grim-faced men with shovels standing next to a pile of dirt, waiting. Then a hooded figure clothed in black and carrying a large scythe approached me. It was the Grim Reaper. He seized me by the shoulders and tried to force me into the grave. Desperately, I clutched at his skeletal arms, fighting him off. But I was losing; I felt I was sliding deep into the pit. Then I awoke, trembling, afraid to go back to sleep.

And at my 60th high school reunion, I was asked to read off the names of our deceased class mates—over one third of our class. For weeks after, I couldn't shake the reflection that kept disturbing my thoughts. I was seeing my classmates as we were when we graduated—young, full of life, with dreams. We were on a broad early evening highway walking toward a mountain. At the top of the mountain was a welcoming beacon of light, showing us the way.

Soon we were walking faster. I began to notice everyone was looking older, some getting gray. We hurried our steps, anxious to get to the top with the light. I started seeing old friends, now in middle age, dropping along side the road. For some reason we could not help them. My best friend staggered and went down, his arm reaching out to me. I did not stop; I rushed on with the crowd.

In time there were fewer of us, the road narrowed. I noticed an old football teammate of mine. He was hunched over, hobbling along with a cane, desperately trying to keep up.

Then I was in the lead. I ran as fast as I could until I heard no one behind me. I stopped and looked back. It was dark and I was alone. I was afraid. I wondered: should I keep going or should I turn back? Why was I hurrying? What would I find at the top of the mountain—at the light?

I think the first dream was, at its core, the fear of death. The second, the hope for a life after death.

Arthur Schopenhauer, the great 18th century German philosopher, said that man's awful fear of death was at the root of innumerable philosophies and theologies; that the average man cannot reconcile himself to death, the end of consciousness, the fearful void, the great unknown.

The three major religions, Judaism, Christianity, and Islam, promise to quell that fear. The basic tenet of each is that there is but one God, the creator of the universe, of heaven and earth, and that to those who believe and follow their precepts, the reward is a blissful afterlife.

But is there but one God, the creator? Andy Rooney, the venerable, erstwhile pundit on the television show, *60 Minutes*, had questions. When asked, he said, "If God created the universe, then who created God?"

W. Somerset Maugham, the English writer of plays, novels, and short stories (1874–1965), tried to answer that question as well. In his memoir, "The Summing Up," written when Maugham was in his 60s, he describes a lifetime search for answers.

Orphaned at a young age, Maugham was raised in England by his uncle, an Episcopal clergyman. Maugham was accustomed to prayers morning and evening and twice on Sundays. He believed that God was all-powerful and that if you had faith you could move mountains.

Maugham had an affliction, a stammer, which brought on ridicule by his school classmates. The night before school, he prayed with all his might that God would take away his impediment. He went to sleep quite certain that when he awoke in the morning he would be able to speak like everyone else. He pictured the surprise of his classmates when he no longer stammered. It was a terrible shock when he discovered he stammered as badly as ever. He began to question his belief.

Maugham came to think that the only God that is of use is a being who is personal, supreme, and good, and whose existence is as certain as two and two make four. But because God allowed evil to exist, God could not be all good. Therefore, Maugham did not believe in God, in heaven, or immortality. But, he reasoned, without God, life had no meaning. Thus he sought to find a meaning for his life.

Maugham studied the great philosophers looking for that one book that would show him the way. He was disappointed. The philosophers, he discovered, contradicted one another—there was no single answer.

Then Maugham looked for a pattern in his life, like his stories with a beginning, middle, and end. He concluded that youth, maturity, and old age was the perfect pattern.

As Maugham approached old age, he was not despondent. He believed he would be liberated from the passions of youth.

As desire was assuaged, he would be free from the pangs of un-requited love, the torment of jealousy, and envy. He would have more time to enjoy art and literature, to take his life to the "end of the chapter."

But life at the end was not pleasant for Maugham. In his final years, he had periods of self-loathing and self-pity. He would sit in a corner muttering angrily to himself and spout obscenities. Then he would break down and sob and say he was a horrible and evil man and that everyone who knew him hated him.

Maugham was not always lucid toward the end. On one oc-casion he greeted his guests as they walked into his drawing room by popping up from the behind the sofa adjusting his trousers. He had defecated on the rug, and scooped up a handful of feces like a child.

Confronted with these indignities, Maugham longed for death, yet at the same time was terrified of it.

Two months before his ninety-second birthday the end came. Maugham's lungs were congested, he was feverish, and his blood was not reaching his brain. He died in the hospital.

Maugham was cremated, as he wanted. Attendants took his corpse and placed it in an oven. As the flames devoured his body, suddenly Maugham sat up as if to protest death—or the fires of hell? The heat had caused Maugham's body to double up.

I have never thought much about God, or of heaven and hell. I accepted the God of Martin Luther, as did my parents and my father's parents. I was baptized and confirmed at St. John Lutheran Church in Montgomery. I was reverential enough to be president of the Luther League, taught Sunday school, sang in the church choir, and ushered on Sundays. Our minister, Reverend Albert Guetzaff, thought well enough of me to get a church scholarship for me to go to Wartburg College in Waverly, Iowa to begin a study for the ministry.

As a kid, I said my prayers at night, and knew the words to say grace at the table. But my faith was more like a capitulation, to follow the line of least resistance. It was more a cultural thing; you went to church because that was what good, decent people did. I felt guilty if I missed Sunday church service.

I left Wartburg College after a year and a half because I could not see myself as a minister. When the Korean War was on, I enlisted in the U.S. Navy. It was in the Navy that I changed. Amongst sailors, many profane and macho, I took on some of their attitudes. I skipped chapel and my prayers at night—although I was careful not to swear and use foul language.

When I was discharged from the Navy, I returned home and met my wife Shirley. We moved to St. Paul, got married in a Lutheran church, and were active in a young couples' group. We moved a lot with my job, but always belonged to a Lutheran church and were active. We got our three boys baptized and confirmed in the Lutheran faith. In 1997, after I retired, we moved to Woodbury, MN and a townhome. We attended services in several Lutheran churches but did not find a new "church home." Eventually, I quit going; I found excuses—guilt no longer compelled me through the door. Now my only church attendance is when a grandchild is baptized or confirmed, or I attend a wedding or funeral—as often in a Catholic church as Lutheran one.

As I near the end of life's journey, I look in the mirror and ask myself, "What do you believe?"

I think again of Somerset Maugham. Although he did not believe in God, he did consider mysticism: that the individual's consciousness continues after death. But he rejected that notion by saying, "For my part I cannot see how consciousness can persist when the physical basis has been destroyed, and I am too sure of the interconnection of my body and my mind to think that any survival of my consciousness apart from my body would be in any sense the survival of myself...The only survival that has any value is the complete survival of the individual."

Then there is spiritualism, the belief that the spirits of the dead live on and communicate with the living. The belief usually requires a "medium" or psychic as an intermediary to interpret the "messages" from the spirit world.

James Van Praagh, a world-famous medium renowned for conveying messages and conversations between the living and the dead in his book, "Talking to Heaven, a Medium's Message of Life After Death," paints an alluring picture of the spirit world. Not only will the spirits of our dead relatives, friends, and loved ones be waiting for us in that other world, but also, he asserts, will be the spirits of our dead pets, our beloved dogs and cats. He goes on to tell the reader how to become a psychic, to communicate directly with those in the spirit world. Mr. Van Praagh states that his work is to help human kind and to spread the love and knowledge of life after death.

26.

How They Died

I look also to my dead relatives for help with my belief—or disbelief. I think of when they died and how they died—when the angel of death came to take them by the hand. Except for one, they all, at least outwardly, professed a belief in God, in a life hereafter. Some were devout, others not.

The most devout was my grandmother on my father's side: Grandmother Mary Bauer. Although Grandpa Conrad did not go to church—he opened the shop on Sunday mornings to serve those who did—Grandma Mary made up for it. She taught Sunday school and was regular in church attendance.

But life was not kind to my grandmother. In 1923, at age 55, she was found to have advanced cancer of the "female organs." Sent home from the hospital to die, Grandma Mary suffered in agony without painkillers. When the torment became intolerable, she sang church hymns and read from the Bible. As an affirmation of her faith, her favorite verse was Job 19:25-27:

> But as for me, I know that my Redeemer lives, and that he will stand upon earth at last. And I know that after this body has decayed, this body shall see God! Then he will be on my side! Yes, I shall see Him, not as a stranger, but as a friend! What a glorious hope!

Grandpa Conrad was more fortunate than Grandma Mary. He lived to be 84 years old and enjoyed good health most of his life—with one exception: he suffered from gastric ulcers. In 1927, at age 63, he went to the Mayo Clinic in Rochester, Minnesota for surgery to correct the problem. The story was that the famed Mayo Brothers, Dr. Will and Dr. Charley were to do the surgery. When Grandpa was wheeled into the operating room, he sat up, looked at Dr. Charley and, being a butcher, asked for reassurance that Dr. Charley was good with a knife. Dr. Charley just said, "Conrad, you just lie down on the table. I can handle a knife just fine." Grandpa had two thirds of his stomach removed, but said it was the best thing he had ever done. After that he could eat and drink anything and never had trouble with ulcers again.

I was with my grandfather when he died. It was a pleasant day on June 4, 1948. My parents, my younger brother Milt, and I were living with Grandpa Conrad in his house on the west side of town at the time. My mom, Milt, our hired man Fred and I were with Grandpa at the noon dinner table. Grandpa was in good spirits, having spent much of the morning watching the workmen installing cement curb and gutter along the street in front of the house.

I still remember that Grandpa Conrad was eating mashed potatoes with creamed peas on top when he started choking. Thinking he had something caught in his throat, Mom started patting him on the back—hoping to dislodge whatever it was so he could catch his breath. It wasn't working. My grandfather, his face darkening, struggled to his feet, gasping for air. Mother and Fred grabbed him under the arms and led him from the kitchen to his bed in the next room. Dr. Fred Westerman was called and upon arriving and examining Grandpa announced, "He's gone. He had a good life and a long one. May we all be so fortunate."

My grandfather never had a chance to be afraid of death. He was called to his "heavenly home" when he least expected it. But even if he had lingered with a terminal disease, I don't think he would have turned to God to help him. He wasn't religious; he never went to church or read the Bible. The only time a prayer was said was when Aunts Esther and Dorothy came and Dorothy said grace in German before a meal.

Grandpa Conrad's oldest son, William Bauer, my Uncle Bill followed in Grandpa's footsteps—he didn't go to church. Struck down with terminal throat cancer at the young age of 46 years, he had plenty of time to think about death, prepare for it, and get religion. But it appears he didn't. Encouraged to start going to church when ill, he refused. As the story goes, he responded, "I'm not going to fill a pew now after all these years—I'm not a hypocrite."

And he did not want to talk about death. Even with his body wasted to less than 100 pounds and his swollen throat burned dark from repeated X rays, he continued to talk about what he was going to do after he got well. Whether he reached out to God on his last day, I don't know.

In contrast, Grandpa Conrad's two daughters, Esther and Dorothy, were close to their mother and from her example gained a religious conviction and faith in God. They were long-time members of Gloria Dei Lutheran Church in St. Paul and professed their commitment to the church and its teachings in both word and deed. Esther chaired the church's Sharing Bank and contributed many hours of personal service and financial assistance to Dorothy Day Loaves and Fishes, a church-supported agency providing hot meals for the homeless. Dorothy sang in the church choir. Together, Dorothy and Esther gave much of their time, talents, and treasure to many church activities during their lifetime.

Esther's death, when it came, did not come easily. It seemed she had to battle cancer for most of the last half of her life. In her fifties, it was uterine cancer, and then in 1986, a persistent anal itch turned out to be carcinoma of the anus, resulting in surgery that necessitated a colostomy. Although onerous, at times embarrassing and an affront to her scrupulous adherence to personal hygiene, Esther joined a support group and carried on. Then in 1992, she was diagnosed with cancer of the left lung. Surgery gave but a temporary reprieve, for in 1993, cancer was found to have invaded her right lung and was deemed to be terminal.

Esther faced the news with a steely resolve. In complete control, she entered the hospice program and chose to remain at home to await death with sister Dorothy to help with her needs. In her small bedroom propped up in bed, she read the morning newspaper, then scribbled a postcard to my parents in Montgomery always ending, "All's well—Thanks be to God!!!" She watched the little chickadees that came to the feeder just outside her window. They seemed to provide her a diverting comfort to what lay ahead.

For weeks, there was a steady stream of visitors to the house: ministers from Gloria Dei Lutheran Church, relatives, and many friends. Ever mindful of social courtesy, Esther instructed Dorothy to provide coffee and dessert to visitors who wished to linger, and to set up card tables so they might play cards or board games. On one occasion, Esther came out of her sick room and asked me to sit with her and watch her favorite movie on video, "Paper Moon," a delightful comedy about a man and young girl, small-time con artists, in 1930s Kansas.

As the days wore on, Esther's breathing became more difficult and pain developed. As I mentioned earlier, morphine was prescribed and helped Esther in those last days. Toward the end Esther was in and out of a coma. I was told that a minister from Gloria Dei came to Esther's bedside and whispered in her ear, "Your mother and father, relatives and friends are waiting for you—there across the river, waving to you."

Esther died on November 16, 1993 without a struggle, carried off on the silken wings of morphine, seemingly at peace. I wonder if she made it across the river—to that wondrous place.

My aunt Dorothy lived a healthy life. At one time or another during her working life, she was a high school science teacher, a nurse, and a physical therapist. She neither smoked nor drank; she never married, never suffered the pain of childbirth or the frustrations of child rearing. Except for a lifelong struggle with narcolepsy, she sailed through life pain-free.

Dorothy's retirement was one of serenity and contentment. Throughout the years, she was active in the church and enjoyed singing in the choir. But it was the summers that gave her the most pleasure. That was when she went to her cabin on Lake Vermilion in northern Minnesota. I have a journal she kept at the cabin for the years 1985–1992. It was filled with little daily comments about such things as the mother duck and her little ducklings that took up residence near her, the beavers that were raising havoc with her small trees, and the comings and goings of Esther, and their many friends who spent time at the cabin. Dorothy loved it so much.

But after Esther's death in 1993, things started to go wrong for Dorothy. The loss of her sister and best friend, the one who handled the day to day management of the house, paid the bills, and protected her from the little aggravations of life, was gone. Soon loneliness and the stress and strain of daily decision-making brought on anxiety and the "blues." Along with the Ritalin Dorothy was taking for her narcolepsy, now she needed the antidepressant Zoloft to get through the day.

Then in 1999, Dorothy suffered a stroke and spent time at the Bethesda Lutheran Hospital and Rehabilitation Center in St. Paul for physical and occupational therapy. But her return home did not go well. She complained of memory loss and seemed afraid to be alone. An agency arranged for 24-hour live-in services to cook meals and ensure Dorothy took her medication. This worked for over a year and a half until her health deteriorated and she needed nursing care.

Arrangements were made for Dorothy to go into the Lyngblomsten Care Center in St. Paul. Although not happy with the idea, Dorothy soon adjusted and seemed to like the place—especially the food. Within a month she gained ten pounds.

For the first few years, Dorothy got along well. She had many visitors: from Gloria Dei, and other friends and relatives. I tried to see her a couple times a month, sometimes alone and other times with my brother Milt. She loved chocolates and flowers and it seemed her room was always well supplied. Every year we held a birthday party for Dorothy with all the things she liked: cake, cookies, etc., and treated her like a "queen." She enjoyed the attention.

Then in the fall of 2004, Dorothy seemed overly concerned about death. She'd ask visitors, "When am I going to die?" Knowing how religious she was, my response was always, "When the good Lord decides," thinking that might help relieve her anxiety. It seldom helped.

In November 2004, the nurse practitioner from Lynblomsten called and said Dorothy was emotionally upset about dying and the doctor wanted to increase her Zoloft to improve her mood. I agreed. The increase seemed to help. But in December, she was having trouble breathing. Diagnosis: slight congestive heart failure. By February, breathing was still a problem and she was given morphine. And along with trouble breathing, Dorothy had urine incontinence and had to suffer the humiliation of having to wear a diaper. We also noticed she was losing weight.

At the February 10, 2005 Care Conference for Dorothy, the nurse said Dorothy was not eating—"purposefully," and was sleeping more with increased forgetfulness. The social worker suggested we contact a hospice program for her.

Arrangements were made for Dorothy to go into the "Hospice of the Lakes" program. Several days later, Shirley and I flew to Phoenix, Arizona to attend our granddaughter's wedding. Soon after, we got a call from a good friend of Dorothy's saying that Dorothy was not doing well. She was calling out, "I want my Mommie—Mommie, help me." A day or two later, Dorothy died.

Like Esther, Dorothy donated her body to the University of Minnesota Medical School. A year and a half later, Milt got Dorothy's ashes back from the U of M. As Dorothy wished, Milt and I arranged for the pastor of St. John Lutheran Church in Montgomery to conduct a memorial service for her. Dorothy's cremains were interred next to Esther's and her parents' with a monument for the sisters that include the words "sisters for eternity."

The only non-believer in my family tree was my grandfather, James Holey, my mother's father. Grandpa Jim was one of the tallest men in town. At 6'4", he always dropped his head at the doorway when coming into our house. A soft-spoken and gentle man, he looked like Abraham Lincoln with long arms and legs, a craggy face, and big farmer's hands with fingers stained brown from heavy cigarette smoking.

Grandpa Jim was a "Free Thinker" and did not believe in the Catholic Church or any religion. This was not unusual as many of the Czech immigrants coming to Montgomery at the turn of the century were affected by free thought, or religious liberalism—as it was sometimes called.

My grandfather married my grandmother, Mary David, a Roman Catholic, in 1910. Grandma Mary gave up going to church, although she saw to it that my mother was confirmed in the Catholic faith.

Grandpa Jim never talked about religion, so I don't know how strongly he felt about it. When he was 88 years old, he fell down in his bedroom and couldn't get up. Grandmother could not lift him. He was taken to the hospital and examined. No bones were broken, but he was very weak through inactivity and old age. He was transferred to a nursing home. Less than a month later, he died.

I have often thought about my grandfather's death, and how he faced it. He never complained about being placed in a nursing home, even though it was still customary to expect relatives to take you in and care for you. He never cried out for help or begged for mercy when his heaving chest demanded oxygen that his damaged lungs from a lifetime of cigarette smoking could not provide. He had been a kind and thoughtful husband and father, and in the end his thoughts were about them and their welfare.

The evening before he died, Grandma Mary and my mother visited Grandpa at the nursing home. He seemed to know the end was near, and looked into their faces intently—as if to burn forever their visages on his brain. As they were leaving, Grandpa raised a feeble hand and gently brushed Grandma's cheek as if to feel the touch of her face for the last time. As they were leaving, he whispered, "Goodbye" in a way that suggested he would not see them again.

Grandfather may have expected death and wished for it that evening, but his body would not give up. His roommate, an old construction worker, said Grandpa died harder than any man he ever knew. All through the night his arms and legs threshed about as he gasped for air—like someone was holding a pillow over his face. Toward the morning, on July 14, 1976, release came.

Grandpa Jim did not believe in God, but would he have died differently if he had? I wonder. He had been a farmer and accustomed to the four seasons. He was in the winter of his life and knew the end must come—as it does for everyone.

The following year, Grandma Mary entered the hospital to have surgery for advanced colon cancer. My mother and I visited her often. Several days before her surgery, Grandma began to reminisce. Seeming to sense the futility of surgery, she recounted her life. For over two visits I listened as almost in a "stream of consciousness" she went over the life she had had with Grandpa, the closeness of their marriage bond, the dependence on one another when in the early years on the farm (before radio, TV and automobile) they had little access to the outside world, rarely seeing their neighbors for weeks on end. It was as if she wanted to savor those days for one last time. Grandma Mary died following surgery.

Although my grandmother did not go to church, she kept one vestige of her Catholic faith—her rosary. She kept it with her at the hospital. Whether it gave her comfort at the end I don't know. But like her husband, Grandpa Jim, one sensed she saw death as the natural end product of life—to be accepted with courage and gratitude.

Up until the last year of his life, my father kept active and enjoyed good health. Although he said he had quit smoking cigarettes and did not buy them, if anyone offered him a smoke or left a pack, he'd puff away. Surprisingly, smoking did not seem to affect his breathing until the end.

But after Esther died in November, Dad seemed to go downhill rapidly. Overnight, it seemed, he'd lost energy, and just walking a few steps to the garage left him breathless. And Mom, now in her 82nd year and never very strong, was having trouble taking care of him.

In January 1994, Mom said she needed someone to come in to help with Dad. We arranged for home health services—a nurse and an aide—to come in on a regular basis. And my father's physician ordered in a portable oxygen tank to help with his breathing. But in April Father developed an infection in his lungs and was taken to the hospital in New Prague. Soon after he was transported to the Mala Strana Health Care Center in New Prague.

It soon became apparent my father would not be coming home. He could not breathe without oxygen and needed full-time nursing care. We celebrated his 91st birthday at the nursing home, but there was no happiness on his face. As the days passed, Dad grew depressed. The only pleasure came one day when a visitor brought a basket with three puppies in it. Dad's eyes sparkled with joy. Shortly after he died.

The funeral for my father was held on August 10, 1994 at St. John Lutheran Church in Montgomery. The casket bearers were my three sons and my brother Milton's three sons.

My brother had done well in life. Milt left home in 1956 and attended Macalester College in St. Paul. Eventually, he got a degree in veterinary medicine, married, served in the U.S. Air Force, and owned and operated an animal hospital in West St. Paul. By 1961, both Milt and I were on our way to successful careers. Dad could see there was no need to hang on to the butcher business.

The funeral for Dad was well attended. I talked to two men who had worked for my father when they were teenagers—while Milt and I were away to college and the U.S. Navy. They both were blue-collar workers. They had had warm relations with Dad, almost like sons to him. They talked about how Dad took them hunting and fishing and took an interest in their lives.

One, I'll call John, tried hard to please Dad. After my father sold the business, John got a job as a meat cutter in the Twin Cities. He raised coonhounds and won prizes in hound competitions. Later, John told me that he had been born out-of-wedlock and raised by his mother. He never knew his father.

At the funeral, John took photographs of my father in the casket, taped an audio of the funeral service, and gave copies to Mom and me. He said he wanted something of my father to remember him by. Mom sold Dad's 1970s Chevrolet Malibu to him for $1,000. It was an old car, but John was thrilled to get it.

Years later, he told me how well the car ran and how he kept it in "mint" condition.

After my father's death, I went through Dad's photo album and found a picture of John with two of his coonhounds. I think Dad found the son he was looking for.

After my father sold the business and retired, he and my mother took trips: a three-month tour of the world in 1961–62, group tours to Hawaii, Cuba, Florida, etc. They enjoyed life.

In 1961, I received a Master's degree in Social Work from the University of Minnesota. Shirley, my wife, and our two sons moved to Rochester, Minnesota where I took a job as a hospital social worker with the state hospital there. A year and a half later, we moved to Bemidji, MN where I was a District Welfare Representative for the Minnesota Department of Public Welfare supervising five country welfare departments. In 1964, I was promoted to supervisor of child protection, responsible for developing regulations and providing consultation to country welfare departments in child protection, services to unmarried parents, foster care services, and homemaker services out of the state offices in St. Paul. It was the year Lyndon Johnson proclaimed the War on Poverty.

Shirley and I bought a house in Cottage Grove, MN, a suburb of St. Paul. I tried to get back to Montgomery as often as possible—to visit with my parents. I had always been close to my mother, and now that I was out of the shop and into a field of work foreign to Dad, he and I remained cordial. We talked about the goings-on in town, the changes in the church services at St. John Lutheran Church, and his hunting forays for deer, coon, and fox.

But we stayed away from politics. My father was a die-in-the-wool Republican, as was my grandfather Conrad Bauer, and thought rewards came from hard work, not handouts. After Dad's death, I found in his personal papers a 1966 editorial from a small-town newspaper in southwestern Minnesota. It was a rant against the growing welfare state—the "beatnicks" and "scabby-faced, long-haired youths" who were sneering at the "old-fashioned virtues of honesty and morality on which America grew to greatness," and the "bearded bums who tramp the picket lines and the sit-ins who prefer Chinese Communism to capitalism—who see no evil in Castro, but sneer at President Johnson as a threat to peace."

My father never understood social work—its role in society, its value. When someone asked my father what I did, he said, "Bart's something like a lawyer."

When I rose to a mid-level manager position with the Minnesota Department of Public Welfare, I became more visible publicly. I was asked to serve on panels and was interviewed about the growing problem of child abuse and neglect, and the increase in the number of children born out-of-wedlock—two programs I supervised. On occasion, I was quoted in the Twin Cities newspapers.

Then it became apparent that I was a member of the growing government bureaucracy changing the face of America. I became an apologist for the liberal changes in federal and state welfare laws. I was a loyal soldier in the nation's War on Poverty.

As time went on, it became more and more difficult to answer the critics. Although I could not admit it publicly, privately I concluded we were losing the War on Poverty. The problems of the poor we were trying to help were growing worse. The welfare rolls were skyrocketing and there were riots in the big city streets—after billions of dollars spent. And I had no answer to my father as to why his taxes were increasing when his income wasn't.

But I think my father was pleased I went to college and got a government job. He could see I was comfortable with paperwork, patient with their demands. I was personable enough, always a smile, and I didn't rock the boat. I was told when my father was asked by a young man about employment, he said, "Get on with the government, it's a lifetime job." I suspect my father thought I would have been a failure as a butcher—too easy-going without the drive to be a success. And I believe he thought I had found a home in big government, enveloped in its sheltering arms, and protected from ever having to meet a payroll.

My father's grave is tucked away in the southwest corner of the St. John Lutheran Church Cemetery about two miles west of Montgomery. He won't be lonely. My mother is buried next to him and nearby are most of his relatives: his father and mother, his grandfather Konrad Bauer, his uncle Joseph, his brother William and wife Anna, and his sisters Esther and Dorothy Bauer.

The cemetery is surrounded by cornfields, and by late August in every direction is a sea of green as high as a man. There are few trees, so about ten years before he died, my father planted two green ash trees next to my parents' grave site. Dad said he wanted a little shade to protect the sod from the harsh rays of the sun. But now he has too much shade. Creeping Charlie has invaded his gravesite, choking out whatever grass is there. Shirley and I have been battling it, but without much luck.

Now that I've come to the end of my life, I often wonder what my father thought of me in his final years. Not long ago, I was sorting through a box of my dad's belongings kept after his death. Inside was a faded and timeworn wallet-sized photograph of Milt and me taken on a boat on Lake Vermilion. It was a close-up and was taken by someone in the boat. My brother and I were in our 20s, and the picture is a good likeness. I was told Dad kept it in his wallet for years, and showed it around with pride whenever asked about his family. That must count for something.

The year 2000 started out well. My 50th high school class reunion brought back happy memories and a chance to see old friends. Shirley and I were in good health and traveling. Then, on the national scene, events turned ugly. The stock market tanked, and we had the attack on the World Trade Center on September 11, 2001. There was fighting in Afghanistan and Iraq, and the violent conflict between Israel and Palestine. We entered an age of suicide bombers and tightened national security.

And on the personal side, there was the passing of my mother and my Aunt Dorothy. After my father died, Mom stayed at home and managed to get along quite well. I made a point of going to Montgomery every Wednesday to do her shopping and spend the night. Then in April 1997, Mom fell in the kitchen and broke her upper arm. She entered the Queen of Peace hospital in New Prague. We did not know it at the time, but it was the beginning of the end for my mother—although the end would not come for another four years.

After several days in the hospital, Mom entered the Mala Strana Health Care Center in New Prague for therapy. By the end of July, she was ready to leave. She wasn't sure she wanted to go home, however, afraid she wouldn't be able to take care of herself—especially with winter coming on. So we found a nice apartment with kitchen for her in the Queens Court apartment complex right across the street from the hospital. Milt and I and our wives moved in a few things Mom wanted from home and bought new furniture. We arranged for Meals on Wheels so she wouldn't have to do much cooking. It all seemed so right.

Not so. Four days later, my mother was back in the hospital. We found out she hadn't been eating (her Meals on Wheels food was piled up in the fridge) and was spending all day in bed—in part due to a long-term dependence on painkillers and sleeping pills. The hospital physician said she could not live alone.

Fortunately, there was a small assisted living facility, REM Health, in the apartment complex with about 10–15 patients providing meals and personal care. We moved Mom in. It provided a wonderful place for her. The staff were small-town people with a "Minnesota nice" attitude. Within a few months, Mom decided she would never go home and wanted to sell the house. Mom gave some things to relatives and friends. We cleaned out the house and put it up for sale. By the spring of 1998, it was gone.

But the next four years would be a struggle for my mother. The infirmities of old age—a bad heart and severe osteoporosis—would prove to be too much. The downward spiral started in May 1998, when Mom felt weak with numbness in her arm and leg. She went into the hospital. Her physician, Dr. Milan Schmidt, said she had suffered heart damage. However, she was able to return to REM Health and assisted living. A month later, she was back in the hospital with pneumonia. She needed skilled nursing care and was taken to the St. Gertrude Health Care Center in Shakopee. By July, she was back at REM Health in New Prague.

Through all this, my mother maintained a positive attitude and kept a clear head. The drugs she was taking for pain relief, anxiety, depression, and sleeplessness were strictly controlled. Her sweet disposition endeared her to the REM Health staff who often said how nice she was to them. And Mom's mind was as sharp as ever. Every morning both Milt and I called her to talk over the day's events. And every Wednesday, we drove down to REM Health and spent a couple of hours visiting with Mom, going over her mail and paying her bills. All financial matters involving her money were discussed with Mom and made with her approval.

But then on September 13, 1999, we had a close call. At 9:45 that night, I got a call from the manager of REM Health. She said my mother had fallen while going to the bathroom and couldn't talk. She thought Mom had had a stroke and should go into the hospital. I agreed and Mom was rushed to the emergency room of Queen of Peace Hospital across the street. I called Milt and we hurried to New Prague.

Milt and I gathered around Mom's bed. She was alert but unable to respond. The young ER physician, Dr. Troy Hanson, said our mother had had a stroke and tests indicated it was due to a blood clot. The left side of her face and left leg were paralyzed. The prognosis was grim. She would spend the rest of her life in a wheel chair, speechless, and having to be fed.

Yet all was not lost. There was a new drug, TPA—they called it the "clot buster"—that if administered within three hours of the stroke could dissolve the clot and restore blood to that part of the brain. If successful, it could lead to a substantial recovery. However, Dr. Hanson, cautioned, there was a three percent chance the drug could kill Mom. We were within the three-hour window of opportunity. But we had to make a decision right away whether to go ahead.

Milt and I looked at Mom. She had heard the whole discussion. Her eyes, wide with fear and hope, seemed to cry out, "Go for it." Milt and I signed papers authorizing Dr. Hanson to go ahead. Soon after administering the drug, Mom started to bleed slightly from the mouth. We grew alarmed. Examination indicated Mom might have had a small cut in her mouth from the fall, and the drug may have opened the cut. We breathed a sigh of relief. We waited. There was no sign of change. At 1:00 in the morning, Milt and I decided to go home. We left our telephone numbers to call if there was any change.

The next morning we returned to the hospital and saw Mom. We could not believe it. She seemed fully recovered—talking with no paralysis—just like she was before the stroke. One of her nurses said Dr. Hanson was so excited at the recovery, he pumped his arm in victory and had three of the older hospital doctors come in to see Mom. The next day, Mom had four visitors from REM, staff and patients. One said, "We love your mother—she's so sweet."

The last two and a half years were tough for my mother. Bent double from osteoporosis, her back in pain from compression fractures to her spine, and her breathing labored because of fluid buildup in her lungs due to a damaged heart, Mom struggled on. Although she remained at REM Health, there were interruptions: four more trips to the hospital and a month in a nursing home along the way.

However, the final episode came the morning of March 3, 2002. I had talked to my mother, as I usually did, about 8:30 that morning. She was in her usual good spirits. Several hours later, I got a call from the manager at REM who said that Mom had fallen and hurt her hip. She was taken by ambulance to the Queen of Peace Hospital. Milt and I rushed down and talked to the ER physician, Dr. Troy Hanson, the same doctor that had given Mom the TPA drug resulting in a miraculous recovery from stroke. He said Mom's hip was broken and would require surgery to repair. Mom was in great pain and asked for something to help with it. We asked Dr. Hanson and he ordered morphine.

Toward evening, Milt and I decided to return home and come back in the morning. Mom was scheduled for surgery in the afternoon. Before we left, we went to see her. I told Mom to get rest so she'd be prepared for the surgery, and that we'd be back in the morning. As we got ready to leave, she reached over and took my hand. "I love you boys," she said.

I squeezed her hand. "We love you too," I replied. I did not know it then, but those would be the last words we exchanged. I think she knew this time she would not recover.

The next morning Mother was under heavy sedation—she did not know we were there. Her surgery was scheduled for 2:30 that afternoon. Dr. Anderson, her surgeon, said he would be putting a steel ball in Mom's hip socket. He was optimistic; thought she would be able to put her weight on that hip soon after the surgery.

After some time in a nursing home for recovery, he thought, she would be able to return to assisted living.

But then came a problem—there was a delay. Finally at 4:30 p.m., the anesthesiologist came out and said Mom was too "fragile" to undergo surgery at the New Prague hospital; she would be transferred to Fairview Southdale Hospital in Edina for the surgery. The transfer was made the next day, but Mom did not have the surgery until the afternoon of March 6th. And there was another complication: Mom's pulse rate was slow and erratic. The doctors thought she would need a heart pacemaker. Mom was on a ventilator and unresponsive.

The next day, Milt and I talked to Mom's cardiologist. The news was not good. He said our mother had had a heart attack during surgery—and the situation was critical.

In the afternoon, Reverend Robert Boda, the visitation pastor from St. John Luther Church in Montgomery, came to see Mom. He said prayers for her. And, although she was still hooked up to the ventilator, tried to talk to her. "But," he said, "she was not responding to me. It was as if she was looking at something over my head."

In the afternoon of March 8th Dr. Norman Chapel, cardiologist, said Mom's kidneys were failing and her blood pressure was low. We reviewed Mom's living will and told Dr. Chapel to continue treating Mom with medication but not use devices to resuscitate her. Dr. Chapel did not hold out much hope for Mom—he said her heart was too damaged.

The end came during the early morning hours of March 9th. At 3:25 a.m. Bridget, the Intensive Care Unit nurse, called and said our mother had passed away. Her struggles were over; she could rest in peace. She had been a wonderful mother to Milt and me—always there for us.

Milt and I went to the hospital and saw Mom for the last time. We gathered her personal effects and drove to Montgomery for a meeting with the funeral director, Greg Schoenbauer, and the minister of St. John Lutheran Church, Pastor Robert Rendahl, to plan the funeral. As was her nature, Mom had looked ahead and planned for her eventual death. Some years before, she had selected the dress she wanted to be buried in, picked out the funeral hymns ("Jesus Calls Us; O'er the Tumult" and "Have Thine Own Way"), and requested the scripture lesson, Psalm 23: "The Lord is my shepherd; I shall not want..."

The funeral was held on March 13th at St. John Lutheran Church in Montgomery with Reverend Robert Rendahl officiating. The pallbearers were Mother's six grandsons. As was customary at the St. John Lutheran Cemetery, bodies were not buried during the winter months when the ground was frozen. So Mom's casket was placed in the cemetery's small mausoleum until the weather warmed.

It was June 11, 2002 when Mother's remains were interred next to Dad's. The day was pleasant and partly cloudy, the birds were singing and the grass was green. Milt and I, our wives, Pastor Rendahl, Greg Schoenbauer and his assistants, and the cemetery manager, Carl Lehman met in the southwest corner of the cemetery where the Bauer family plots were located.

With Mother's casket next to the gravesite, Pastor Rendahl conducted the burial service. Shirley had brought a yellow rose and she placed it on the casket. As we said our last goodbyes and turned to go, I noticed a large mechanized truck with two men in the cab—the "gravediggers." They were waiting until we left and Greg gave them the go-ahead to lower the casket into the grave and cover it over. I thought a moment; that's how it goes. We're leaving and Mom is staying. And then one day it will be my turn to stay.

But Mom is not forgotten. For weeks after her death, every morning about 8:30, I'd reach for the telephone to call her. It took a long time to get out of the habit. And there isn't a day goes by that something doesn't come up to remind me of her: one of her favorite phrases ("Well, they'll just have to work it out"), her favorite movie ("The Letter" starring Bette Davis—a favorite picture of mine I've been watching over and over recently), and the osteoporosis I'm treating (My physician says I inherited the tendency from my mother). And then there are the two prominent personality traits Mom passed on to me: the need for solitude, and a fear of offending others. I'm very much my mother's son.

Esther Pauline Bauer (on left) and sister Dorothy Marie Bauer (on right) at their home, 229 Macalester Street, St. Paul, 1944.

My grandparents James and Mary Holey on their
42nd wedding anniversary at their home at 214
Elm Ave in Montgomery, 1952.

Milt and I with sons at Funeral Home. Pa requested all six of his
grandsons be his casket bearer. His wish was granted. My three sons
are in the back row and Milt's in front.

In Memory of

MILTON B. BAUER

May 28, 1903 - August 5, 1994

FUNERAL SERVICE
Wednesday, August 10, 1994
2:00 p.m.
St. John Lutheran Church
Montgomery, Minnesota

CLERGYMAN
Rev. Terje Hausken

INTERMENT
St. John Lutheran Cemetery
Montgomery, Minnesota

CASKET BEARERS
Jeffrey Bauer   Eric Bauer
Scott Bauer   Steven Bauer
Brent Bauer   David Bauer

Arrangements by
Schoenbauer Funeral Home

26.

Is There a Hereafter?

THERE—THAT'S HOW they died. Whether they believed in God and a life hereafter or not, they all ended the same way—in a hole in the ground with a minister saying words from the Bible to send them on their way.

I never asked any of my relatives if they believed in God; I never thought to ask. But if I had, I think all, except for my grandfather, James Holey, who wasn't a Christian, would have said yes. For who of them would have had the courage to say no, even if they had doubts?

My mother, however, was asked the question. When she was in her 80s, shortly before she died, Mom told me a friend of hers at the assisted living facility was dying of terminal cancer. She asked Mom, "Rose, is there a heaven?" Mom's answer was, "I don't know. No one has come back to tell us." My mother said no one had ever asked her about God or the hereafter before, and she answered as honestly as she could. I'm like my mother—I have never been asked. But if I were, I would probably answer as she had.

Sometimes I wish I had the conviction as some others do: that there is a God, that one day when I die, I will rise again and go to that heavenly kingdom to be with my loved ones, to walk amidst the green pastures in peace and harmony. It would make death something to look forward to—to be in "that better place." But unfortunately, I don't have that faith.

Now at age 80, death still is a mystery to me. It was a mystery when I was five years old and watched my father slash the throat of the calf and saw it die—and it is now 75 years later. Yet I contemplate how death will come to me.

Will death come to me like it came to Grandpa Conrad, when he was feeling good and enjoying a nice meal—unexpectedly—or will it entail months of suffering like my grandmother Mary Bauer and my uncle Bill Bauer? Will I face it with a steely resolve like my Aunt Esther, or will I whimper like my Aunt Dorothy, "I want my Mommie, Mommie, help me"? Will I fight death to the end like Grandpa Jim and my father, or will I welcome a lethal dose of morphine?

Will I see death as the Grim Reaper and fight him off as I did in my dream, or will I see death as an Angel of Mercy, to envelop me in her loving arms as a young child seeks the warmth of a security blanket? And will there be anyone sitting next to my bed when the end comes, to hold my hand, to comfort me? Will it matter to me?

I have always been interested in famous last words, the dying person's thoughts at the end. Some are funny: "I should never have switched from Scotch to Martinis" (Humphrey Bogart, actor, d. January 14, 1957). "Either that wallpaper goes, or I do" (Oscar Wilde, writer, d. November 30, 1900).

Some are fearful: "You are going to hurt me, please don't hurt me, just one more moment, I beg you!" (Madame du Barry, mistress of Louis XV, d. 1793 at the Guillotine).

Some show bravado: "Take a step forward, lads. It will be easier that way" (Erskine Childers, Irish patriot, d. November 24, 1922. Executed by firing squad.).

Others are angry: "You sons of bitches. Give my love to Mother" (Francis "Two Gun" Crowley, d. 1931. Executed in electric chair.).

And others defiant: "I'd like to thank my family for loving me and taking care of me. And the rest of the world can kiss my ass" (Johnny Frank Garrett, Sr., d. February 11, 1992. Executed by injection, Texas.).

There are those who are resigned: "I'm bored with it all" (Winston Churchill, statesman, d. January 24, 1965 before slipping into a coma).

And those who are contemplative:

The time comes in the life of each of us when we realize that death awaits us as it awaits others, that we will receive at the end neither preference nor exemption. It is then, in that disturbed moment, that we know life is an adventure with an ending, not a succession of bright days that go on forever. Sometimes the knowledge comes with the repudiation and quick revolt that such injustice awaits us, sometimes with fear that dries the mouth and closes the eyes for an instant, sometimes with servile weariness, and acquiescence more dreadful than fear.

~ *William March, American author and highly decorated U.S. Marine in World War I, d. May 15, 1954.*

And finally those who approach death expectantly: "Now comes the mystery" (Henry Ward Beecher, evangelist, d. March 8, 1887).

What will my last words—last thoughts—be? Will anyone care?

Then you wonder what happens after you die. I am a Christian, but my faith is not strong. I don't know if all my relatives and friends will be waiting for me "on the other shore." I recall a minister whispering into my Aunt Esther's ear, as she lay in bed comatose, dying of cancer. "They are all waiting for you across the river, waiving to you, welcoming you home." I don't know if Esther heard it, or if she did, whether it helped ease her mind.

Could the prophets, the wise men of old. The James Van Praaghs, be right? Should I try to reach out to my family in some way after my death, to speak to them from heaven or the spirit world? And would they want to hear from me?

Epilogue – 2012

LOOKING BACK OVER 80 years, you wonder if it has all been worth it. You ask questions in your mind. Have you made a constructive difference for having lived? Have you been a good husband, father, a productive worker, a useful citizen? You tote up all the pluses and minuses. But can you look at yourself clearly? Perhaps the final score will have to be made by someone else.

And you think about a legacy—what will you leave to your relatives, your blood kin, after you are gone? Will it amount to a few stocks in a mutual fund, some bonds, a little cash in a savings account, or will it be something more? Something that will last?

Perhaps my only immortality will be in the hearts and minds of those who remember me. Maybe this book will carry something of myself to those who read it, continue to speak for me. Down the line is a future generation, one I'll never know, who might find my life and times of some interest. I hope so.

CPSIA information can be obtained at www.ICGtesting.com
Printed in the USA
LVOW10s1752160815

450302LV00005B/99/P